ASPEN PUBLISH

Friedman's
Practice Series

Constitutional Law

SECOND EDITION

Edited by

Professor Joel Wm. Friedman

Tulane University Law School
Jack M. Gordon Professor of Procedural Law & Jurisdiction

 Wolters Kluwer

Law & Business

AUSTIN   BOSTON   CHICAGO   NEW YORK   THE NETHERLANDS

To contact Customer Care, e-mail customer.care@aspenpublishers.com, call 1-800-234-1660, fax 1-800-901-9075, or mail correspondence to:

Aspen Publishers
Attn: Order Department
PO Box 990
Frederick, MD 21705

Printed in the United States of America.

1 2 3 4 5 6 7 8 9 0

ISBN 978-0-7355-8620-8

About Wolters Kluwer Law & Business

Wolters Kluwer Law & Business is a leading provider of research information and workflow solutions in key specialty areas. The strengths of the individual brands of Aspen Publishers, CCH, Kluwer Law International and Loislaw are aligned within Wolters Kluwer Law & Business to provide comprehensive, in-depth solutions and expert-authored content for the legal, professional and education markets.

CCH was founded in 1913 and has served more than four generations of business professionals and their clients. The CCH products in the Wolters Kluwer Law & Business group are highly regarded electronic and print resources for legal, securities, antitrust and trade regulation, government contracting, banking, pension, payroll, employment and labor, and healthcare reimbursement and compliance professionals.

Aspen Publishers is a leading information provider for attorneys, business professionals and law students. Written by preeminent authorities, Aspen products offer analytical and practical information in a range of specialty practice areas from securities law and intellectual property to mergers and acquisitions and pension/benefits. Aspen's trusted legal education resources provide professors and students with high-quality, up-to-date and effective resources for successful instruction and study in all areas of the law.

Kluwer Law International supplies the global business community with comprehensive English-language international legal information. Legal practitioners, corporate counsel and business executives around the world rely on the Kluwer Law International journals, loose-leafs, books and electronic products for authoritative information in many areas of international legal practice.

Loislaw is a premier provider of digitized legal content to small law firm practitioners of various specializations. Loislaw provides attorneys with the ability to quickly and efficiently find the necessary legal information they need, when and where they need it, by facilitating access to primary law as well as state-specific law, records, forms and treatises.

Wolters Kluwer Law & Business, a unit of Wolters Kluwer, is headquartered in New York and Riverwoods, Illinois. Wolters Kluwer is a leading multinational publisher and information services company.

Check Out These Other Great Titles

Friedman's Practice Series

Outlining Is Important But PRACTICE MAKES PERFECT!

All Content Written By *Top Professors* • 115 Multiple Choice Questions • Comprehensive *Professor* Answers and Analysis for Multiple Choice Questions • *Real Law School* Essay Exams • Comprehensive *Professor* Answers for Essay Exams

Available titles in this series include:

Friedman's Civil Procedure

Friedman's Constitutional Law

Friedman's Contracts

Friedman's Criminal Law

Friedman's Criminal Procedure

Friedman's Property

Friedman's Torts

ASK FOR THEM AT YOUR LOCAL BOOKSTORE
IF UNAVAILABLE, PURCHASE ONLINE AT *http://lawschool.aspenpublishers.com*

About the Editor

Joel Wm. Friedman

Tulane Law School
Jack M. Gordon Professor of Procedural Law & Jurisdiction,
   Director of Technology
BS, 1972, Cornell University; JD, 1975, Yale University

Professor Joel Wm. Friedman, the Jack M. Gordon Professor of Procedural Law & Jurisdiction at Tulane Law School, is the lead author of two highly regarded casebooks — "The Law of Civil Procedure: Cases and Materials" (published by Thomson/West) and "The Law of Employment Discrimination" (published by Foundation Press). His many law review articles have been published in, among others, the Cornell, Texas, Iowa, Tulane, Vanderbilt, and Washington & Lee Law Reviews.

Professor Friedman is an expert in computer assisted legal instruction who has lectured throughout the country on how law schools can integrate developing technologies into legal education. He is a past recipient of the Felix Frankfurter Teaching Award and the Sumpter Marks Award for Scholarly Achievement.

TABLE OF CONTENTS

CONSTITUTIONAL LAW
ESSAY EXAMINATION
QUESTIONS

CONSTITUTIONAL LAW ESSAY EXAM #1

QUESTION #1

In response to increasing medical knowledge about the genetic source of obesity, Congress enacts and the President signs the "Obesity Rights Act" (ORA). The statute reads as follows:

§1. Findings

The Congress hereby finds that the obese are subject to unreasonable and unfair discrimination in employment, given prejudice against and misunderstanding of, the condition of obesity. The Congress also recognizes that a desire to earn a profit may require a business to consider the physical attributes of certain members of its work force, and that this is a legitimate consideration.

The Congress also finds that obesity is not a legitimate tool for determining the capability of any person to contribute to an efficient workplace.

§2. Discrimination

It is a violation of federal law for any employer to discriminate unreasonably against any person based on the person's weight, except where weight is a bona-fide occupational requirement and where all reasonable attempts have been made to accommodate the person.

§3. Definitions

"Employer" means any person, partnership, corporation or other business entity, or state or subunit of state government, that employs any person.

§4. Relief

Any person may sue to enforce the provisions of this act in any federal court where venue is proper. A court may order damages, back pay, or other relief, as appropriate.

§5. Regulations

(a) The U.S. Department of Labor is authorized to promulgate regulations to enforce these provisions. Violations of any valid regulation shall be considered violation of federal law.

1. Adams v. Baker

Albert Adams, a junior auditor for the State of Baker, is fired for being obese. He sues the state and the state's head auditor under the law, requesting back pay, damages, and an injunction against the head state auditor forbidding him from firing or demoting Adams. What constitutional defenses could Baker make to the lawsuit and the requests for relief?

2. Confederation for the Prevention of Obesity Discrimination (CPOD) v. Department of Labor

Meanwhile, the Department of Labor promulgates the following regulation:

Reg A: A "bona-fide occupational requirement" is any requirement that, in the eyes of a reasonable employer, is reasonably necessary to prevent a loss of business or profit, taking into account reasonable customer preferences.

The Confederation believes that this regulation is far too lenient, and contravenes the intention of the statute. On the day the regulation is promulgated it sues the Department of Labor. Does it have standing?

3. Everett v. Fair Skies Airlines

Edwina Everett is a flight attendant for Fair Skies, based in Chicago, which is also the airline's corporate headquarters. Edwina brings a lawsuit against Fair Skies, claiming a violation of Illinois employment law. Illinois employment law is all common law, and has evolved to the point at which, according to one recent court decision, "any unreasonable discrimination which robs the people of the state of the talents of willing workers, is a violation of Illinois law." Edwina sues Fair Skies in state court on the state law cause of action. What federal constitutional arguments would Fair Skies have in defense?

You may assume the following:

1. During its consideration of the ORA, Congress heard evidence that, as a psychological matter, people make assumptions about people's self-control and discipline based in part on whether they are obese. Congress was also told that, in a public opinion poll, 67% of Americans said they would be uncomfortable working with an obese person.
2. Three individuals testified to Congress that they were fired from jobs, one from a job with New York state government, one with a large corporation, and one with a small business, based solely on their obesity, despite achieving good performance reviews.
3. The CPOD was formed "to fight, in the legislatures, the courts, and in public opinion, all forms of discrimination and stereotypes about, and oppression of, obese persons."

QUESTION #2

As it becomes more and more popular for drug companies to advertise their name-brand drugs on television, Congress becomes concerned that individuals will demand that their doctors prescribe them rather than generic drugs, or perhaps even demand drugs they don't need at all, thereby unnecessarily raising the cost of health care. Thus, Congress enacts the Drug Advertising Act (DAA), which reads as follows:

Section 1: No drug company may advertise a particular prescription drug to the public on television, radio, or print or electronic media.

Section 2: States are hereby directed to consider and enact laws prescribing good codes of medical practice for doctors, to alert them to the problems that arise when their patients demand certain drugs. Any state that fails to enact such a law within one year of the date of this statute's enactment will lose 25% of federal Medicare funds. The Department of Health and Human Services (HHS) will determine when states have complied with this requirement.

Section 3: Any person may sue to enforce any violation of Section 1. Such a suit may be brought in the state court of general civil jurisdiction where the plaintiff or defendant is a resident, or the state where such advertising took place. Such a court may order any relief it deems appropriate.

1. *Anderson v. BigPharma*

Andy Anderson, a pharmacist in New York, sues BigPharma, a New York-based corporation, for a drug advertisement that was placed in the New York Observer. Anderson argues that, as a pharmacist, his professional expertise has become devalued because customers no longer seek him out for advice on prescription drugs, instead relying on television advertisements. Anderson sues in a New York court. Assume that New York courts follow federal standing law. Does Anderson have standing to sue? Assuming he does have standing, what constitutional arguments would BigPharma have against Section 1?

2. *Colorado v. Dept of Health and Human Services*

After HHS determines that the State of Colorado has not complied with Section 2 and thus cuts off their funding, the State sues, arguing that Section 2 is unconstitutional. What arguments might it have?

QUESTION #3

Ned is a mid-level manager for Ajax Forms, a privately owned company that supplies forms to private and public entities. Ned is also African-American. Ninety percent of Ajax's revenues come from government contracts with the State of Texas; those contracts specify in detail the quality and performance requirements for the forms the government purchases from Ajax, but otherwise don't discuss Ajax's operations.

Ned has been at Ajax for 5 years. It is company policy to employ mid-level managers on one-year contracts, but in the last 20 years only two out of 300 mid-level managers have left because the company has decided not to renew their contracts. The company employment manual reads as follows:

"Mid-Level Managers: Ajax believes in the stability of its mid-level management team. Thus, any mid-level manager who is happy and productive and an asset to the company can expect to remain employed with Ajax."

The manual also reads as follows:

> "Dismissals: Any dismissal for any reason is final unless the company itself decides to reconsider the case. In case of a dismissal, the employee shall have the right to submit written comments and materials tending to show why he/she should not be dismissed, but has no right to an oral hearing until after an adverse dismissal decision. After that decision the dismissal is effective; should the oral hearing lead to the employee's rehiring, he will NOT be paid the lost salary. Oral hearings, if requested, shall be held within six months of any firing decision."

One day, as his fifth one-year contract was nearing its end, Ned was summoned to his supervisor's office. He thought this meeting would be for the purpose of signing his next contract, but instead the supervisor told him that "he just wasn't working out" and that his current contract would not be renewed.

Ned files suit against the company. What constitutional claims could he make? You may assume that a witness who was a government procurement expert would testify that if Ajax didn't supply the government with its forms, the government would probably just print them itself. You may also assume that Ned has five years of written performance reviews that he submitted to the company as part of its initial firing decision.

CONSTITUTIONAL LAW ESSAY EXAM #2

QUESTION #1

Your client is Baker's Books, a large general-interest bookstore operating in Austin County in the State of Alabama. Among its broad variety of books, the store carries adult-oriented material. Specifically, it carries the following:

    a. Books that describe, without pictures, children engaging in sexual activities.

    b. Books that describe, in words and photographs, the history of sex in various world civilizations; these books include historical photos and photos of contemporary models demonstrating various methods of achieving orgasm adopted or prized by various cultures in history.

    c. Books put out by a publisher called "Man's World." Man's World publishes books that espouse the view that "women are put on this earth to give sexual pleasure to men." These books consist of stories and pictures of men using women in various settings rife with sexual innuendo, with the woman being shown in degrading and humiliating positions or roles. The pictures sometimes show men and women in the nude, but the primary focus is on men's stories about their female conquests, with pictures depicting fully clothed men "conquering" partially clothed women.

    d. Books put out by a publisher called "Sexart." Sexart publishes books consist of stories and pictures designed to titillate and arouse sexual interest; the name "Sexart" comes from their trademark practice of depicting ultimate sex acts taking place in front of a reproduction of a famous painting.

    1. The local district attorney brings suit to enjoin the bookstore from carrying these books.

Meanwhile, a protest crowd gathers around the store. Colleen Collins, a local anti-pornography activist who organized the protest, gives a fiery speech in which she calls pornography "an abomination," and further states, "before we can be purified we must purge all abominations from our midst." During the speech Collins' assistants pass out a newsletter called The Divine Way, which has an article alleging (incorrectly) that Bob Baker, the bookstore owner, is a pedophile and Satan worshipper. The newsletter got this information from a source on the Internet, which referred to someone actually named Bob Booker, who was arrested for distributing pornography (not child pornography) the previous week in Oregon.

The crowd gets more and more excited as Collins continues to speak. At the climax of her speech, a member of the crowd throws a brick through the glass door of the store, exclaiming, "Cast the demons out!" That action precipitates a melee, in which members of the crowd forcibly enter the store and damage its contents.

    2. Collins is arrested for inciting a riot.

    3. Baker sues The Divine Way for libel.

Analyze these claims and their likely outcomes.

QUESTION #2

In response to mounting concerns about unscrupulous telemarketing tactics, Congress enacts the "Fair Marketing Act" (FMA). The FMA reads as follows:

§1. Findings

The Congress hereby finds:

Telemarketing can bring many economic benefits to the nation, but only if properly and fairly conducted.

Unscrupulous and unfair telemarketing erodes public confidence in the economic system, with serious effects on national prosperity.

§2. Unfair and Unscrupulous Telemarketing Prohibited

It shall be a violation of federal law for any individual or business entity to propose a business transaction to a stranger over the telephone, if such proposal is conveyed in a misleading or fraudulent manner.

§3. Federal Fair Marketing Agency

There is hereby created within the existing Federal Trade Commission an office entitled the Federal Fair Marketing Agency ("Agency" or FFMA). The head of the FFMA shall be appointed by the President for a five-year term, and shall be removable by the President before the end of that term only for good cause, or by Congress, via impeachment.

The FFMA shall have the authority to promulgate regulations implementing Section 2 of the statute.

The FFMA shall also have the authority to adjudicate claims, whether brought by its own prosecutors or by private parties, that an individual or business entity has violated Section 2. FFMA adjudicators shall not have the power to enforce their own orders. To enforce an order, the party prevailing before the FFMA shall apply to any federal court where venue is proper. The results of such adjudications may be appealed to any federal court where venue is proper. When a federal court reviews an appeal from an FFMA order, or a request to enforce such an order, it shall review the agency's fact findings under the "weight of the evidence" standard, and shall review its legal conclusions de novo.

§4. Legislative Oversight

Congress may overturn any regulation promulgated by the FFMA, upon a majority vote of both the Senate and House of Representatives.

Identify and analyze the constitutional issues raised by this statute. You may assume that the head of the FFMA is an "inferior officer" of the United States.

QUESTION #3

The World Trade Organization meeting in Seattle a few years ago engendered a great deal of protest. For years, Seattle has had an ordinance on the books banning protests in the hotel district (where many of the delegates were staying) between 11 p.m. and 8 a.m., to ensure that hotel guests not be disturbed during the evening, and also to guard against the possibility of protesters and onlookers getting drunk and turning violent. Billy Zoom is a protester who, with some friends, violates the

11 p.m. protest curfew. During the protest, Billy climbs on top of a car and, with great fanfare, burns his passport as a protest against globalization. After being taken into custody by Seattle police for violating the curfew, he is charged by federal authorities for willful destruction of a passport, a federal offense.

    1. Billy contests both charges. What First Amendment defenses does he have?

The unrest causes the mayor of Seattle to declare a state of emergency, requiring that businesses refrain from selling potentially dangerous items such as toy guns and handcuffs; the mayor's order states that contracts for such sales "are null and void during the period of this order." Carl Carlson owns a novelty store downtown; the decision means that he could not complete a large sale of handcuffs he had contracted to sell to a local theater group for a performance. The theater group goes elsewhere to buy their props.

    2. Carl sues the City of Seattle. What claims could he make and how successful would they be?

Meanwhile, Dana Danson, another protester, leads a group of 20 protesters to the gate of the Boeing aircraft plant outside Seattle. They erect a platform and start shouting at the workers coming off the day shift. The workers at first ignore the protesters, but soon Dana and his followers start yelling epithets at individual workers picked at random or any who made eye contact, calling them Nazis, "angels of death and destruction," and "stupid sheep." Two of the workers respond by scuffling with the protesters. Plant security calls the sheriff, who arrests Dana for inciting a riot.

    3. What First Amendment defenses would Dana have? Would they be successful?

CONSTITUTIONAL LAW ESSAY EXAM #3

QUESTION #1

After several horrific instances of animal cruelty receive major press coverage, Congress passes and the President signs the "Federal Animal Cruelty Act." The statute reads as follows:

§1. Findings
   The Congress hereby finds the following:
   1. Instances of cruelty toward cats and dogs erode the humane and moral foundations of America.
   2. In particular, instances of such cruelty harden all Americans' attitudes toward pets. In turn, this hardening attitude lessens the interest Americans have in having rewarding long-term relationships with their pets. This shift in turn reduces the demand for care and nourishment of cats and dogs, and ultimately reduces the demand for such animals generally.
   3. The sale, care, and nourishment of cats and dogs is a multi–billion-dollar industry in the United States.

§2. Prohibition on Unnecessary Cruelty
   No person shall inflict unnecessary cruelty on a companion animal.

§3. Definitions
   1. "Unnecessary cruelty" means any intentional infliction of physical harm that is not part of legitimate training or disciplining or humane euthanasia.
   2. "Person" means any natural person, business association, or state or any instrumentality or arm of a state.
   3. "Companion animal" means a dog or a cat, including dogs and cats that are used for work activities.

§4. Training; Penalties
   Any person found to have engaged in unnecessary cruelty shall, on the first offense, be ordered to undergo appropriate animal care education, as to be determined by the judge. On the second offense, the judge, should the conditions warrant, shall order the offender to undergo an anger management class and/or to serve at a local humane society, but under no circumstances shall any second offender be made to spend more than 16 hours completing the required class or service. On third and subsequent offenses, the offender shall be fined by an amount not to exceed $500 per occurrence. If the offender is not a natural person, the person subject to the animal care education, anger management, or humane society service orders shall be the individual who actually ordered or committed the act of unnecessary cruelty; however, the non–natural-person offender shall remain liable for any fines.

§5. Enforcement
   1. Enforcement of this action shall be performed by county animal control authorities and county law enforcement, both of which shall promptly investigate any legitimate complaints of unnecessary cruelty.

2. In addition, any person witnessing or having proof of an act made illegal under this statute may bring suit to enforce this statute against any person who has violated the statute.

3. Suits alleging violations of this statute shall be brought in any state court that normally has jurisdiction to hear civil misdemeanors under that state's law.

After the statute is enacted, Peter Peta goes bike riding at Malibu Canyon State Park in California. He watches as a detachment of State Park Police officers conduct a drug sweep of a homeless encampment, using drug-sniffing dogs. After one of those dogs snarls at a homeless person, a police officer hits the dog with a nightstick.

Later in his ride, Peter notices Sylvester Stallone, a private individual, beating his Golden Retriever with a pair of boxing gloves.

The next day, Peter files two lawsuits in Los Angeles County Superior Court. One is against Stallone, and the other is against both the California Park Police and the officer that hit the dog during the drug search.

1. What argument(s) can Stallone make that the statute exceeds Congress' Article I power? Explain why each argument would or would not succeed.

2. Aside from the argument(s) Stallone can make, what additional argument(s) can the Park Police make that the statute cannot regulate how it treats its dogs? Explain why each argument would or would not succeed.

In answering these questions, you may assume the following:

a. Peter has standing to sue.

b. Police dogs come within the definition of "companion animals."

c. The California State Park Police is an arm of the State of California.

d. California has not explicitly waived any sovereign immunity.

e. Under California law, civil misdemeanors are heard in Superior Court.

QUESTION #2

After a record-hot summer, Congress and the President decide to do something about global warming. Congress passes, and the President signs, the "Global Warming Study and Control Act" ("the GWSCA"). The statute reads as follows:

§1: Findings

The Congress hereby finds that global warming may present a potentially serious long-term problem for the United States and the rest of the world. The consequences of doing nothing in the face of a threat such as this are serious. However, the scientific evidence is still not clear, and activities that might contribute to global warming provide many benefits for Americans, including economic prosperity and increased levels of health and welfare.

§2: Definitions

. . .

(d) "Person" includes any individual, corporation, other business association or government body, whether federal, state or local.

§3: Study and Action
(a) The National Oceanic and Atmospheric Administration (NOAA) is hereby directed to conduct an intensive, multi-year study of global climate change, its consequences and causes. This report shall be delivered to the Congress no later than January 1, 2015.
(b) No person shall emit so-called "greenhouse gases" if it is shown, based on solid scientific evidence, that such emission contributes to global climate change and is unnecessary to the continued prosperity and health of the American people.
(c) The Environmental Protection Agency (EPA) shall promulgate regulations to implement Section 3(b).

In response to the same hot summer, the California Legislature enacts the "Greenhouse Gas Reduction Act." It reads as follows:

§1: Findings
The California Legislature hereby finds that greenhouse gases contribute to global warming. As the largest economy of any state in United States, it is the responsibility of the State of California to take the lead in ensuring reductions of these dangerous gases.

§2: Emissions Limitations
No person in the State of California shall emit any more greenhouse gases in any year than such person emitted in the calendar year 2008. The California Environmental Protection Agency (Cal-EPA) shall promulgate regulations to account for unusual factors, such as a business not being in existence in 2008, or running its emissions-producing operations at unusually low levels in 2008.

Anderson Plating, a manufacturer in California whose operations emit greenhouse gases, sues to prevent enforcement of the California law. What constitutional claims could it make?

QUESTION #3

I. Introduction

In late 2009, the American public is shocked to hear of isolated cases of individuals dying after eating tainted duck. Although at first attributed to poor sanitary conditions in restaurants, or failure to cook the duck properly, subsequent investigation reveals the presence of a disease entitled "Anataidae Neurosa." The media quickly dubs it "Daffy Duck Syndrome (DDS)," owing to its obvious similarity to Mad Cow Disease.

In response, Congress enacts, and the President signs, the following statute:

§1. Title
This statute is entitled the Safe Duck Consumption Act.

§2. Findings
The Congress hereby finds:
1. That rational and economically reasonable regulation of duck breeding and raising is necessary to ensure the safety of the duck supply destined for human consumption;

2. That duck production will be hampered both by lax regulation, which would undermine the public's confidence in the safety of eating duck, and overly strict regulation, which would impose unnecessary and ruinous costs on duck producers; and,

3. That, given the disparate conditions of the duck-raising industry in the various states, state governments are best suited to ensure the safety of ducks destined for human consumption.

§3. Duck Safety Regulations

Every duck producer in the United States who intends any part of his duck flock for consumption by any human shall ensure that, to the extent feasible taking into account costs of compliance, its flock is free of Anataidae Neurosa.

§4. State Regulations; Failure to Regulate

A. Every state in which there is a flock of ducks kept by any person who intends any part of said flock for consumption by any human, shall designate an agency of the state government to be responsible for ensuring that said flock is free of Anataidae Neurosa, to the extent feasible, taking into account costs of compliance. Each such agency, in turn, shall promulgate regulations that best achieve that goal. Such regulations shall be submitted to the U.S. Department of Agriculture (USDA), which shall then determine whether the regulations satisfy the standard set forth in §3. Regulations approved by the USDA shall be considered federal law.

B. The Secretary of Agriculture shall monitor state compliance with this statute, and enforce any failures to comply as provided for in §5.

§5. Suits Against State and Federal Governments

Any person may sue any state or federal entity for non-compliance with any part of this statute, including failure to properly enforce this statute. These suits may be brought in either federal or state court. Such court may award damages or fines and/or issue an injunction or order any other relief it deems proper.

★ ★ ★ ★

II. Subsequent Activity

After the statute is enacted, the Governor of California announces that, pursuant to the statute, the State Department of Agriculture (CalAg) is responsible for performing the tasks specified in the federal law. CalAg promulgates the following regulation:

Reg D-1: Keepers of duck flocks in California must test their flocks for Anataidae Neurosa every six months, and destroy any duck found to be infected, and to quarantine the rest of the flock for three months.

The USDA is considering the California regulations when the following lawsuits are brought.

★ ★ ★ ★

III. The Lawsuits

Plaintiff: Mary Hartman

Mary Hartman, a resident of San Diego, becomes severely ill after eating her annual birthday meal of Peking Duck at her favorite Chinese restaurant. An investigation reveals that the duck was contaminated with DDS, and came from a flock near Santa Barbara.

Pursuant to §5 of the statute, Mary sues the state of California and the Director of Cal-Ag, alleging that its regulatory program fell below the federal standard, as more stringent regulation would have been economically feasible, and that more stringent regulation would have prevented her illness. Mary seeks damages amounting to $5 million for pain and suffering, medical bills, and lost wages, and for an injunction requiring California to promulgate tougher guidelines for duck raising and to enforce those tougher guidelines strictly.

1. Can Mary sue in federal court? What about state court? Under what conditions or limitations? If it's relevant, you may assume that CalAg is an arm of the State of California.

Plaintiff: American Association of Poultry Producers

At the same time, the American Association of Poultry Producers (AAPP) is unhappy with the statute. The AAPP is an association of poultry (chicken, duck, quail, and geese) producers whose by-laws state that it was created to "promote the interests of poultry producers in the United States by ensuring safe, efficient, economical and humane methods of poultry raising." The day after the statute becomes law, the association sues the United States Secretary of Agriculture, seeking an injunction against implementation or enforcement of the statute.

2. Assuming the AAPP has standing to sue, can it challenge the statute now, or does it have to wait for an enforcement action against one of its members?
3. Assuming the AAPP can sue now and has standing to make any legal arguments it wishes, what arguments can the AAPP make that the statute violates the Constitution? How successful will it be?

CONSTITUTIONAL LAW ESSAY EXAM #4

QUESTION #1

In the town of Retirement World, California, pet owners start reporting mysterious cuts on their dogs. Investigation leads to a quasi-Christian religious cult, the Church of the Blood of Christ (CBC). Further investigation leads the police to discover that the CBC has as a ritual, relatively minor in the religion's dogma, something called the "leaching of the animals of Christ," in which small pets are given a minor cut by exactly seven believers, and their blood ritually spilled to the ground. This discovery shocks the small retirement community, which consists of privately owned land governed by a corporation, in which each resident owns shares proportionate to the size of his or her house lot. The town, in addition to home lots, has two main streets with storefronts, a post office, and a County Sheriff substation. The roads are privately owned, but link up to the state of California's road system at either end of the town. A sign at the end of each of the main roads reads, "Private Property: Residents, Invited Guests and Those on Official Business Only." At the next meeting of the town's Board of Directors, the Board enacts the following town ordinance:

> "No cutting of live animals shall be allowed except in cases of pest destruction, animals under the care of a doctor, humane euthanasia, and hunting."

1. In response to the ordinance, the CBC sues.

While the lawsuit is pending, the CBC refrains from performing the ritual described above, but instead, performs a mock-up of that ritual, in which stuffed animals are used along with red Kool-Aid to simulate blood. To increase the town's awareness of their presence, the cult requests a parade permit to perform the mock-up ritual every Sunday afternoon for the next month. In response, the town's Board enacts the following ordinance:

> "No parades of more than five individuals will take place within the next six months, and such parades as are allowed must include only the marchers and no props of any types."

2. The CBC amends its lawsuit to challenge this second ordinance.

What claims can the CBC make? How likely is it that they will prevail?

QUESTION #2

In 2009, Congress enacts the following statute:

§1. Findings
  The Congress hereby finds the following:
    1. The health costs associated with treating sickness caused by secondhand smoke are considerable, and have restricted economic activity by inflating

insurance premiums and thus limiting the expansion of small businesses, which have been the largest source of economic growth over the last decade.

2. The American Association of Asthmatics (AAA) has worked ceaselessly to improve Americans' respiratory health.

§2. Smoke-Free Public Spaces; Smoking Areas

A. Except as provided for in subsection (B), smoking is hereby prohibited in all places open to the public and not subject to ample natural ventilation.

B. For all places subject to subsection (A)'s ban, reasonable provisions shall be made to ensure, to the extent feasible taking into account the paramount concerns for non-smokers' health, that smokers be able to smoke without allowing secondhand smoke to migrate into the rest of the public place.

§3. Violations; Lawsuits

A. Any owner or operator of a public space covered in Section 2 who violates any provision of this law shall be liable as follows:

1. A court shall first require the violator to submit to the court a plan to place itself in compliance with the law. If the court rejects the plan, it shall offer the violator a second chance to develop a compliance plan.

2. If the court rejects the second plan, or if at any time the violator refuses to cooperate in the development of a compliance plan, the court shall have the authority to impose its own plan and to impose a fine of up to $500. In developing its own plan the court shall allow input from the plaintiff on the plan's content.

3. Violation of a compliance plan will result in a fine of up to $1,000 per day for each day of non-compliance.

B. Any person may sue to enforce this law, in any federal court where venue is proper or in any state court of general jurisdiction.

In that same year North Dakota enacts the "Smokers' Health Act" (SHA). It reads as follows:

§1. Findings

The North Dakota Legislature finds that smokers are often forced out of doors to smoke, with the result that in winter many smokers suffer serious respiratory infections due to exposure to bitterly cold air.

§2. Equal Access

People who wish to smoke shall have equal access as non-smokers to all places open to the public.

The North Dakota Department of Education posts the following statement in the lobby of its headquarters building in Bismarck:

"This lobby is open to all individuals conducting business with the State Department of Education. Pursuant to the Smokers Health Act, smoking is permitted in this lobby."

Al B. Weezin, who has asthma, conducts business in the Education Department's building as part of his delivery service. An activist on behalf of asthmatics, Al belongs to the AAA. He calls the AAA's national office, and complains about the Department's policy.

1. Can the AAA sue?

2. In what court can it sue?

3. What relief can it seek?

4. Assuming a court could hear the claim, is the federal statute valid? Is it valid as applied to the State Department of Education?

QUESTION #3

In 2009, advances in cloning technology make it scientifically feasible to clone a human being from a minute piece of one or a combination of two living persons' DNA. In response, in March 2010, the California Medical Association (CMA) enacts Ethical Canon 2010-02. The Canon reads as follows:

Section 1: The CMA hereby finds that cloning, at the current stage of the technology, is scientifically uncertain and morally repugnant. Doctors' advice that cloning is an appropriate or available method of reproduction has caused, and, if allowed to continue, will continue to cause, human suffering and anguish.

Section 2: Any doctor found to be
  (1) performing or assisting the performance of cloning, or
  (2) counseling the technological feasibility of cloning as a method of reproduction, or
  (3) discussing the availability of cloning services in other states or nations, shall be stripped of his or her license to practice medicine in California.

Andy Anderson and Art Acton are a gay couple living in Fresno who wish to be parents, and who view cloning as the most appropriate way to procreate without involving a stranger to their relationship, such as a surrogate mother or the biological mother of an adoptive child.

1. Anderson and Acton sue the CMA.

Bob Baker is a medical doctor, licensed by the CMA to practice medicine in California. One day he receives a certified letter from the CMA, informing him that his license to practice medicine has been suspended for violating Ethical Canon 2010-02. The letter informs him that he is immediately to cease and desist the practice of medicine. It also informs him that he has the right to contest the determination, as noted in the CMA's The California Doctor's Handbook of Doctors' Rights and Responsibilities. Baker has made a fortune in the stock market, but continues to practice medicine because he loves it.

2. Baker sues the CMA, demanding an oral hearing before his license is suspended.

Chris Collins is also a doctor, specializing in alternative parenting. He stages a media event in his L.A. office in which, in front of television cameras, he advises a patient of the availability of cloning in Mexico. The next day, he receives a letter from the CMA stripping him of his license to practice medicine for violating Ethical Canon 2010-02.

3. Collins sues the CMA.

Identify and analyze the constitutional claims that could be made by Anderson, Baker, and Collins. Be sure to analyze whether any of the three could even claim that the CMA was subject to the Constitution. If you conclude that the CMA is not required to comply with the Constitution, proceed with your analysis as if it were. Don't worry about any claim Collins may have to a hearing before his license is suspended.

To assist your analysis, reprinted on the following pages are excerpts from the following documents:

1. California Health and Safety Code Section 500.02.
2. A partial transcript of the March, 2010 meeting of the CMA's Board of Trustees, at which Ethical Canon 2010-02 was adopted.
3. Excerpts from the letter from the CMA to Bob Baker.
4. Excerpts from The California Doctor's Handbook of Doctors' Rights and Responsibilities.

CALIFORNIA HEALTH AND SAFETY CODE

§500.02: California Medical Association

The California Medical Association (CMA), a non-profit California corporation, is hereby delegated the sovereign authority to regulate the practice of medicine in California. In exercising this authority, the Legislature directs the CMA to develop and implement a system of medical licensing, ethics and discipline in order to uphold the highest ethical and professional standards of the profession.

EXCERPTS FROM THE LETTER FROM THE
CMA TO BOB BAKER

The CMA's determination that you have violated Ethical Canon 2010-02 is based on the following evidence:

1. A statement by Harry Mata, your receptionist, that on several occasions you orally discussed cloning with patients;
2. A statement by Karla Kampa, one of your patients, that she heard you discussing cloning over the telephone, while she was in the examination room next to your private office;
3. A handwritten note, on your prescription pad, with the address of Clone Technologies, Inc. (CTI), and the name of a known cloning expert at CTI, dated after the enactment of Ethical Canon 2010-02, delivered to CTI by Tamara Tompkins, a patient of yours.

EXCERPTS FROM THE MINUTES OF THE BOARD OF
TRUSTEES OF THE CALIFORNIA MEDICAL ASSOCIATION

Secretary: The next item on the agenda is the proposed ethical canon regarding cloning.

Trustee Able: We all know we have to do this. The technology is outrunning us; we have to do something now to stop a stampede toward cloning.

Trustee Baker: I don't know. You know, cloning could really be a godsend to so many people who want to be parents of their own biological children, without bringing a surrogate into the process. Surrogacy is so emotionally draining, it's morally questionable itself, and the surrogate backs out more than half the time.

Trustee Charlie: All that's true. And adoption isn't always possible, especially for single people and gay people. We all know the legislature has made adoption difficult for gay people. This is just another hurdle for them.

Able: Look, this isn't about gays, and it isn't about preventing people from becoming parents. It's about a technology that's not ready for the public yet, and about preventing unscrupulous doctors from profiting from desperate people's attempts to do anything to have their own biological offspring.

Charlie: Is that why the proposal includes a gag rule?

Able: Yeah. Our concern is with the effects doctors' speech on cloning will have on people taking terrible risks with human life. I'd be the last person in the world to advocate stopping speech because I disagree with the message. But this speech will cause enormous harm. You know how much people trust their doctors, especially when they're desperate and looking for advice about this sort of thing.

Baker: Well, I've certainly heard of patients hearing about cloning from their doctors, then running out and finding the first clone clinic they can find and jumping right into the process. It's certainly led to a lot of heartache.

Charlie: I'm also concerned about the process here. Usually a proposed ethical canon is supposed to be circulated to the medical community and other interested parties for comment for six months before we vote. Can I ask the Secretary if that's been done here?

Secretary: Ma'am, this proposal was circulated for comment two months ago. Yes, normally ethical canons are circulated for comment for six months before a vote is taken. When this one was circulated, it was noted that the comment period would be shorter.

Able: And we all know why that was. This is a time-sensitive thing. People are running out to get cloned, and doctors are setting up shop all over the state to perform those services. If we don't stop it now, something awful will happen.

WHEREUPON, a vote was taken, and the proposal was enacted by a unanimous vote, and codified as Ethical Canon 2010-02.

EXCERPTS FROM THE CALIFORNIA DOCTOR'S HANDBOOK OF DOCTORS' RIGHTS AND RESPONSIBILITIES

Section 1: Introduction
Welcome to the fraternity of California medicine. As a licensed California doctor you bear a large number of rights and responsibilities, as explained in this handbook. . . .

. . .

Section 4: License Revocation: Terms
Holding a license to practice medicine in California entitles you to all the rights and privileges accorded doctors by California law. You can expect to continue to hold your California medical license as long as you meet the criteria explained below:

A. You remain mentally and emotionally competent to practice medicine, as determined by the CMA;

B. You comply with all ethical directives and canons promulgated by the CMA; and

C. You do not provide the CMA with other good cause to terminate your license.

Section 5: Procedures for License Revocation

Should the CMA decide that you fail to meet one or more of the criteria listed in Section 4, the CMA will notify you that your license has been revoked. At that point your name will be placed on the CMA's official website of doctors whose licenses have been revoked.

Should you disagree with the CMA's determination that you are no longer fit to practice medicine in California, you may appeal the CMA's determination. Appeals will be heard by a committee of doctors appointed by the CMA.

Such appeals will be decided on the basis of documentary submissions; under no circumstances will an oral hearing be held. Decisions will be rendered within six months of the filing of an appeal and the supporting documentary evidence. Should you be dissatisfied with the results of that process you may request a review by the CMA's Board of Trustees. Board of Trustee review will include an oral hearing, at which witnesses may be called, if desired.

Should either the initial appeal or Board of Trustee review result in a decision in your favor, your license will be returned to you, and your name will be removed from the CMA website's list of doctors whose licenses have been revoked. . . .

Section 9: Signature and Acceptance of Terms

Please sign in the space below, tear off the lower half of this sheet, and mail it to the CMA. Mailing us your signature on this form signifies that you have read, understood, and accepted the terms and conditions in this Handbook.

[You may assume that Baker signed and returned the signature form.]

CONSTITUTIONAL LAW ESSAY EXAM #5

QUESTION #1

In the spring of 2009, the trustees of the Louisiana State University (LSU) consider whether to discontinue or revamp the school's affirmative action policy. Excerpts of a memo to the trustees, detailing the history of the school's admission policies with regard to race, is attached as Exhibit A to this exam. The trustees eventually decide on a new policy, attached as Exhibit B. The minutes of the Board of Trustees meeting at which the change was adopted is attached as Exhibit C.

1. In the spring of 2010, Alan Ackerman, a white student rejected for admission to LSU for the Fall 2009 entering class sues, alleging that the new admissions policy violates the Equal Protection Clause.

The new policy causes a great deal of consternation on campus. In the fall of 2009 Black Students United at LSU (BSU-LSU) begins a series of rallies, every Monday at 10 a.m., commemorating the day and time the trustees adopted the new policy. The first few of these rallies are non-violent, if noisy. However, starting in October the rallies take on an angry tone, after a group of counter-demonstrators begins attending the periphery of the rallies. The counter-demonstrators are also non-violent, but their presence adds tension to the rallies.

At the October 22 rally, Bob Bride, a professor in the Political Science department, gives a fiery speech, talking about the history of civil rights protests, and having as its theme the idea that minorities in the United States have gained what rights they have only as a result of forcing the white majority to confront the nation's history of discrimination. Toward the end of his speech, with the crowd getting emotional, he says the following:

> "Blacks have never won any rights without shoving the Constitution in whites' faces. Compromise has been tried. It doesn't work. Politeness has been tried. It doesn't work. Patience has been tried. Patience has been tried. Our patience is OVER!"

At that point the crowd begins chanting, "No more patience. Shove it!" One of the members of the crowd, a student at the law school, takes his constitutional law casebook out of his backpack and throws it at one of the counter-protesters, yelling "Here's the Constitution! Shove it!" The counter-protester suffers a broken nose. The incident touches off a melee in which individuals on both sides are injured, several seriously.

2. Bride is arrested for inciting a riot. He claims the First Amendment as a defense.

After the riot, the University president comes under extreme pressure to calm the situation. He issues the following directive:

> Directive 2009-56: To minimize race-based misunderstandings and to promote tolerance and a spirit of inclusiveness, all student organizations shall adopt

and enforce racial non-discrimination policies with regard to membership and attendance.

> 3. BSU–LSU, whose by-laws state that membership is restricted to African-Americans, sues to have Directive 2009-56 declared unconstitutional. Excerpts from the by-laws are reprinted as Exhibit D.

Analyze these constitutional claims. Which, if any, are likely to succeed? Why or why not?

EXHIBIT A
MEMORANDUM

February 18, 2009

From: Office of Research, Board of Trustees
To: The Trustees
Re: A History of LSU's Admissions Policies with Regard to Race

    . . . It is a sad but undeniable fact that LSU's admissions policies have historically been influenced by race. From the school's founding in 1848 until 1964, African-Americans were officially barred from attending LSU. In 1964 the prohibition was dropped, but the first African-Americans did not matriculate until 1966. Vestiges of official discrimination continued until 1972, when the last official arm of the university, the marching band, dropped its refusal to admit African-Americans.

    . . . In 1973 the University began official outreach efforts to the African-American population, which culminated in the adoption of the current affirmative action policy, in 1977.

EXHIBIT B

Press Release, dated March 20, 2009

Today the Louisiana State University announces a new undergraduate admissions policy. Previously the school had used a 1-100 scoring system for undergraduate admissions based on SAT scores and high school grades, with Louisiana residence, African-American heritage, and one or more relatives as LSU alumni each providing an automatic 10-point increase in an applicant's score. The new admissions policy, effective for applications for admission for the Fall 2002 entering class, is as follows:

    "LSU seeks to admit an accomplished and talented entering class, representing the diversity of experiences both of Louisiana residents and Americans generally. Applicants will be scored on a 1-100 scale. Of the possible 100 points, 75 are based on SAT scores and high school grades — that is, a perfect SAT score and 4.0 GPA will lead an applicant to be scored at 75. The remaining 25 possible points will be scored based on the non-quantifiable criteria that, in the view of the admissions officer, will both ensure that the entering class contains students with special experiences and talents, and seek to compensate students who have had to surmount unusually large hurdles in the course of their education. Special experiences and talents include foreign travel or living experience, special artistic or athletic potential, military or significant public service, and unusual life experiences. Hurdles include, among other things, economic, cultural or social hardship and physical or emotional handicap."

EXHIBIT C

Excerpts of the Minutes of the Board of Trustees Meeting, March 10, 2009

Chairman Anderson: The next item on the agenda is the new admissions policy.

Trustee Baker: This policy is gibberish. What's going on here?

Trustee Carter: You know good and well what it is. Race-based affirmative action is on its way out. The Supreme Court is clearly hostile to it. We've got to do something.

Trustee Davis: Well, what does "something" mean? Just reinserting a race preference under the smokescreen of "cultural or social hardship?"

Anderson: Not necessarily. That preference includes all kinds of things. Cajuns would probably get a preference, if they grew up in a Cajun community. So would poor people. God knows there are lots of poor whites in this state.

Davis: Well, yeah, but everyone knows that proportionally speaking, blacks are much poorer than whites in this state. A preference for "economic hardship" cases would catch a much higher proportion of all black applicants than of all white applicants, even if, on a raw numbers basis, there would be more poor white applicants than poor black ones.

Carter: We all know that. But we have to do something. We have a legacy of discrimination in this state. Even LSU itself. You all got the memo from the research office. And everyone knows how crummy the elementary and secondary schools are in black neighborhoods in this state.

Anderson: Yeah, and look, we've been thinking about revamping our admissions policy for years now, to be more nuanced about who we should give preferences to. You can't look at the hardship criterion in isolation; there are lots of ways to get a preference here. And remember, the new policy never ever says that "race gets you extra points." It might not. If you were a middle class black kid with no special experiences, you wouldn't get the preference.

Baker: I'm so not convinced. We stopped discriminating almost 40 years ago. We have nothing to do with the situation in the elementary and secondary schools. And one more thing: Why isn't this admissions policy going to the university President first, for his formal input? Isn't that the way we usually do things?

Carter: It is, you're right. But we don't have time. We need to decide this now, so we can change the application packets and train the admissions staff. There's nothing nefarious about what we're doing.

Anderson: Maybe it's time we voted.

Whereupon, a vote was taken and the new policy enacted by a 3-1 vote.

EXHIBIT D

Excerpts from the By-Laws of BSU-LSU

. . .

III. Membership: BSU-LSU seeks to ensure that African-American students at LSU can socialize and discuss issues of importance to the African-American community in an atmosphere that is comfortable and free of race-based pressure. BSU-LSU believes that a distinct African-American perspective on issues exists, and that development of that perspective requires discussions within the community. To that end, even though BSU-LSU intends to work with other progressive organizations on and off campus, and even though some social gatherings will be open to all members of the University community, member-ship in and attendance at BSU-LSU meetings is restricted to African-Americans. Any African-American student at LSU is eligible to be a member or attend any meeting.

QUESTION #2

The City of Los Angeles has decided to clean up and renovate the Hollywood area of the city. As part of its plan, the City has enacted Ordinance 12345, reprinted below.

ORDINANCE NO. 12345 OF THE CITY OF LOS ANGELES

ENACTED MAY 1, 2009

The Council of the City of Los Angeles hereby finds the following:

1. The stretch of Hollywood Boulevard between Cahuenga and La Brea Avenues is world famous as the center of the global entertainment industry and a vital part of the historical heritage of the City of Los Angeles; and

2. Millions of tourists visit this area every year, contributing billions of dollars to the local economy; and

3. Uncontrolled commercial development in Historic Hollywood has led to the establishment of retail businesses inconsistent with the historical heritage and tourist focus of the area; and

4. Such retail establishments often advertise in crass, distasteful ways that reduce the sense of history and sophistication normally associated with Hollywood; and

5. Such uncontrolled development has also led to a concentration of theaters and arcades offering sexually oriented materials; and

6. Such inappropriate retail businesses and theaters/arcades reduce the attractiveness of the area to tourists and residents alike, to the detriment of all; and

7. In particular, heavy concentrations of sexually oriented businesses lead to a concentration of public drunkenness, prostitution, and other crimes; and

8. Political marches that take place in the area cause divisiveness, tend to be noisy and disruptive, and generally detract from the family atmosphere necessary for any vibrant tourist district.

Therefore, the City Council today enacts this ordinance, which may be referred to as the "Hollywood Improvement Act of 2009," or "HIA."

§1: Hollywood Boulevard between Cahuenga and La Brea Avenues is hereby designated "Historic Hollywood."

§2: The following businesses are hereby prohibited in Historic Hollywood:

a. Retail operations in which more than 50% of sales volume consists of purchases under $10.00, unless the retail operations are primarily (1) dry cleaners, (2) restaurants or cafes, or (3) grocery stores;

b. Retail operations in which more than 50% of sales volume consists of purchases of radios, CD players, or tape recorders; and

    c. Retail operations offering tattooing or piercing, except that piercing may be offered as a free service if the customer buys a piece of jewelry costing over $100.00.

§3: Any business that earns more than 5% of its sales revenue through the sale or rental of sexually explicit goods or services, including exhibition of sexually explicit videos or pictures, shall be located at least 1,000 feet from any other such business.

§4: The police department shall give no permits for marches or demonstrations in Historic Hollywood, if such march or demonstration has a political theme, regardless of the particular political issue sought to be discussed or the viewpoint sought to be expressed.

★ ★ ★ ★

The following parties are affected by the ordinance.

    Boulevard Investments (BI) is a corporation that owns several buildings on this stretch of Hollywood Boulevard. BI rents out storefront space to the small gift shops and electronics stores that would be most adversely affected by the ordinance. BI has several current rental contracts with such stores that must be terminated because the ordinance makes it impossible for the lessors to carry out the kind of business contemplated in the lease.

    Sam Shady owns two adult-oriented book and video stores on Hollywood Boulevard. The two stores are within 200 feet of one another.

    The Center for Immigrant Rights (CIR) is an organization that sponsors an annual march down this part of Hollywood Boulevard. The march centers on CIR's demands for reform of government policies toward immigration and immigrants. CIR likes to stage its marches on Hollywood Boulevard because of the media coverage it thereby enjoys and because the march helps politicize the sizable immigrant population in Hollywood.

    The City Attorney asks you to evaluate any possible constitutional claims these parties may have. Evaluate whether such claims are likely to be successful. Assume that the City of Los Angeles, as a subdivision of the State of California, is subject to the same constitutional constraints as a state.

QUESTION #3

    In 2009, the Decatur, Illinois school district expels two students for fighting at a football game. The students, Anderson and Bennett, were African-American. The school board decided to expel the students involved, on the ground that they violated the school district's rules for student conduct. Expulsion means that they will be sent to a state-run school for violent students, where they will complete their high school studies unless and until readmitted to their regular schools.

    1. Billy Bennett, one of the expelled students, requests that before he gets expelled he be allowed a chance to explain his conduct to the Board, and to cross-examine eyewitnesses to the fight. The Board denies his request.

During the period of this controversy, the city enacts an ordinance prohibiting "marches on public streets expressing an opinion on either side of the expulsion issue." Nevertheless, the Reverend Jesse Jackson, a nationally known civil rights leader, leads a march down a quiet residential street leading to the high school, with the crowd chanting slogans in favor of reinstating the expelled students.

When the crowd reaches the school, Jackson gives an impassioned speech demanding that blacks not be kept out of the educational process. The crowd begins to chant, "We want in, we want in." After a few minutes, members of the crowd begin to push against the locked doors of the school, yelling, "We want in." Soon the crowd breaks through the door, destroying it and several trophy cases in the lobby.

    2. After the rally, the police arrest Jackson for violating the "no march" ordinance and for violating an Illinois law that makes it a crime to "incite a riot."

The melee causes a great deal of tension in Decatur. In response, the city orders that businesses near the school allow only two students in at one time, to minimize the possibility of fights breaking out. This is bad news for Elsie Etawanda, who runs an ice-cream stand near the school that is a well-known student hangout. Elsie loses a great deal of business and is forced to cancel several short-term supply contracts with ice cream suppliers, to her economic detriment. Elsie's total yearly revenues are approximately $500,000 and the store's net income is $50,000; the contract cancellations cost her a total of $5,000.

    3. Elsie sues the city.

Identify and analyze the constitutional claims that may be made by Billy and Elsie. What are the relevant legal tests, and how do they apply? What First Amendment defenses does Jackson have to his arrest? What is the likely outcome of these lawsuits?

In analyzing these claims, the following materials, provided below, might be helpful:

    1. Excerpts from the student handbook; and
    2. Excerpts from the minutes of the City Council meeting at which the Council enacted the ban on protest marches.

If it is helpful, you may make the following assumptions:

    1. The Decatur School Board is an arm of the State of Illinois.
    2. The Decatur High Student Handbook was written and is enforced by the School Board.

EXCERPTS FROM THE STUDENT HANDBOOK DECATUR HIGH SCHOOL DECATUR, ILLINOIS

INTRODUCTION

Welcome to Decatur High! As a validly enrolled student you have the right to a first-class education here, as long as you're between the ages of 14 and 18, are making satisfactory progress toward your diploma, and don't commit any offense for which you can be expelled. We hope you enjoy your four years here.

        ★ ★ ★ ★

Part III: Expulsion
A. Grounds for expulsion

Expulsion from Decatur High shall only be imposed for the following offenses:
1. Significant violent behavior;
2. Flagrant dishonesty; or
3. Gross negligence showing disregard for the safety of students, faculty or staff.

B. Procedure for expulsion

If the School Board determines that any grounds for expulsion exist, it shall order the student's expulsion. Upon expulsion, the student may, after half the semester has passed, seek review of the expulsion decision. In support of that review the student may seek an oral hearing before the Board. At that hearing the student and/or his parents may speak, and he may present whatever written information may be relevant to his reapplication, including any information relevant to whether the student actually committed the offense for which he was expelled.

★ ★ ★ ★

Part X: Acceptance of Rules and Regulations

By signing below, you indicate your acceptance of the rules and regulations set forth in this handbook.

Sign here: _____

[You may assume that the students involved in this hypothetical signed the handbook.]

EXCERPT FROM THE MINUTES OF THE CITY COUNCIL MEETING OF DECATUR, ILLINOIS
APRIL 5, 2009

Clerk of the City Council: The next item on the agenda is the proposed ban on marches relating to the high school expulsion issue.

Councilman Smith: We've got to do something. We have media running around the city like crazy, making us the laughingstock of the country.

Councilman Henry: I agree. But I have just one question. This isn't going to get us into trouble, is it? I mean, we're not stopping the anti-expulsion people from protesting while allowing the pro-expulsion folks to march, right?

Councilwoman Theodore: That's right. This ordinance bans all rallies and marches about the expulsion issue, regardless of the position the marchers take.

Henry: Well in that case it's OK with me, as long as it isn't discriminatory like that.

Whereupon a vote was taken and the ordinance was enacted by a unanimous vote.

CONSTITUTIONAL LAW ESSAY EXAM #6

QUESTION #1

In June 2009, Congress, alarmed by reports of tainted pet food, enacts the "Pet Custodial Responsibility Act of 2009" ("Act" or "PCRA"). The Act reads as follows:

§1. Findings
  Congress hereby finds the following:
  A. The pet boarding and custodial industry is a multi–billion-dollar industry accounting for significant interstate commerce.
  B. Americans derive a great deal of satisfaction and happiness from their relationships with their pets.
  C. Opinions from the federal courts regarding the rights of animal owners to compensation for harm done to their pets have significantly undervalued the importance Americans attach to their relationships to their pets.

§2. Standard of Care for Animal Custodians
  Any person or business entity entering into a custodial care arrangement for the custodial care of a pet shall use special care when feeding such pet. Any such person or business entity shall be liable for both material damages and emotional distress damages caused by any harm deriving from the custodian's choice of dangerous or tainted food.

§3. Dispute Resolution
  A. Claims for the damages specified in Section 2 shall be heard by the Board of Companion Animal Health Claims ("Board"), a tribunal to be staffed by persons chosen by the Secretary of Commerce. Members of the Board shall serve five-year terms.
  B. The Board has the exclusive power to hear all claims arising under this statute and any other legal claims related to a plaintiff's claims under this statute. In resolving such claims the Board shall decide all questions of law and fact.
  C. Appeals of a Board decision shall be made to the United States Circuit Court of Appeals for the circuit where the custodial arrangement was created. That court shall uphold any fact-findings and legal conclusions made by the Board unless such findings or conclusions were clearly erroneous.
  D. The Court of Appeals shall have sole power to enforce any judgment of the Board.

Subsequent Facts

In August 2009, Paula Prentiss left her home in Eugene, Oregon for a weekend trip to her mother's house, also in Oregon. On the way she left her dog, Varmint, with her friend Dan Douglas, who also lives in Eugene, and who agreed to watch Varmint as a favor to his friend, for no charge. The Saturday night of that weekend Dan killed, plucked, and roasted on an open fire one of the chickens he keeps in his backyard, which he feeds with rainwater and chicken feed he distills from sunflowers that grow naturally on his property. After eating the chicken, Dan fed Varmint a chicken bone. Varmint choked on the bone and died immediately.

Paula brings a claim before the Board seeking damages under the Act. Dan immediately sues in federal court, claiming that Congress does not have the constitutional authority to regulate his particular conduct. Put another way, Dan argues that the Act cannot be constitutionally applied to him, given the particular facts of his case. The court rules on Dan's motion in September 2009.

1. How should the court rule?

In addition to making the argument above in his federal lawsuit, Dan attaches an Oregon common-law tort trespass claim against Paula (you can assume that the federal court has jurisdiction over this claim). This claim alleges that Paula had certified to him that Varmint was flea-free, but that in fact he was infested with fleas, with the result that his property will have to be fumigated, thus destroying the organic environment he had created for himself. Paula asks the court to dismiss this claim and direct him to raise it before the Board as a counterclaim to Paula's claim. Dan opposes Paula's motion, arguing that, even if Congress has the power to regulate his particular conduct in this case, the Constitution nevertheless prohibits the Board from hearing and deciding his state-law claim. The court rules on Dan's motion in September 2009.

2. How should the Court rule?

QUESTION #2

Anthony Armstrong and Bob Baker are a gay couple living in Cheddar County, Wisconsin. They want to become foster parents, and one day they go to the local foster parent agency, Hilldale Family Services, Inc. Hilldale is a private non-profit entity dedicated to the welfare of children in Cheddar County, and is run by a fundamentalist Christian church. Hilldale administers a foster parent program and orphanage. This facility, the only one of its kind in the county, takes in county children the State of Wisconsin has deemed wards of the state, for example, when a court finds parents to have been abusive. Hilldale also takes in U.S.–citizen children of illegal immigrants who are being deported, as a purely private relationship between it and the parents.

Hilldale operates under a license from the State of Wisconsin. Receipt of the license is based on the facility's compliance with state regulations dealing with conditions of care and the level of investigation the facility must perform before placing a child with foster parents. The regulations state, among other things, that a facility like Hilldale must determine "that, in its [the facility's] opinion, the prospective foster parents will provide appropriate and loving care for the child."

Hilldale refuses the couple's request to become foster parents. Its rejection letter cites Armstrong's and Baker's sexual orientation, which it describes as "a quality that renders you, in our opinion, unfit to be entrusted with the care of a child."

Analyze whether Armstrong and Baker have a meritorious claim that they have been denied their rights under the Due Process Clause of the U.S. Constitution.

QUESTION #3

Section 500.01 of the State of Iowa's Family Law Code reads as follows:

Section 500.01: Child Custody, Preferences

When a married couple with a male child divorces without agreement on child custody, the court shall award custody based on the best interests of the child. The court shall presume, absent clear and convincing evidence to the contrary, that the best interests of a child lie in the recommendations made by the Iowa Family Council (IFC). If no IFC recommendations directly apply, the court shall make an independent determination of what lies in the best interest of the child.

★ ★ ★ ★

Sonia Samuels and her husband, Bobby, divorce without agreement on custody arrangements for their son, Zach. After the divorce, Sonia comes out as a lesbian and soon moves in with her female partner. Six months later, during the proceedings in family court, the judge awards Zach to Bobby, citing only the IFC's publication, Recommendations for Child and Family Placement in Iowa Courts, 2007.

Sonia appeals the judge's decision, arguing that it violates her rights under the Equal Protection Clause. Analyze her claim.

The judge's decision is reprinted below in Exhibit A. Excerpts from the IFC's 2007 report are reprinted below in Exhibit B. Excerpts from the minutes of the IFC's December 1, 2006 meeting, where the 2007 recommendations were finalized, are reprinted below in Exhibit C. A memo to the Board from the IFC's Archivist, dated November 10, 2006 and supplied to the Board before the December 1 meeting, is reprinted below in Exhibit D.

If it helps, you can assume that the IFC is a non-profit private entity whose membership is open to mental health care professionals, licensed psychologists, and family counselors who have an interest in the promotion of healthy families.

APPENDIX A

In the Matter of Zach Samuels
Family Law Court, Iowa City, Iowa, October 1, 2007

Smith, J.:

In the absence of any specific factual evidence regarding the best interests of Zach, and based on Section 500.01 of the Iowa Family Law Code, I hereby award custody of Zach to his father, Bobby Samuels.

[signed]

Jack Smith, Judge of the Family Law Court

APPENDIX B

Excerpts from Recommendations for Child and Family Placement in Iowa Courts, 2007 (Des Moines, IFC Press, 2007)

. . .

Recommendation 5: When a male child is the sole subject of the custody issue, preference should be given to the husband, unless the wife has either

(1) remarried with or

(2) is otherwise in a stable, committed relationship with, a man, in which case this recommendation is neutral as between the mother and the father.

IFC Comment to Recommendation 5: The IFC continues to believe that the presence of a male authority figure is crucial to the complete socialization of boys, and thus reiterates this recommendation, which has been made by the IFC every year since its recommendations began in 1912. (Comment amended to this current language, Oct. 20, 1975).

APPENDIX C

Excerpts from minutes of the December 1, 2006 meeting of the IFC Board of Directors

Clerk: The next item on the agenda is the adoption of Recommendation 5.

Trustee Alice Anderson: I have to repeat the opposition I expressed last year to this measure. It's sexist and mean-spirited. Can anyone imagine that in this day and age we're still calling for a preference for the father of a male child simply because he's a man?

Trustee Bob Baker: I support continuing the recommendation. It's been there ever since the state started incorporating our recommendations, way back in 1912. It's worked well and there's no reason to change it.

Anderson: No reason? There's every reason to change it. It's utterly sexist to believe that a male child can't thrive without a male parent figure in the house. Lots of women have raised boys just fine on their own.

Trustee Chris Conrad: Well, there's conflicting evidence on that, isn't there? I mean, some studies show that boys socialize better when there's a male role model in the household.

Anderson: And other studies show just the opposite. And we haven't ever done a serious study of the issue in the 30 years I've been on this board.

Baker: It's worked well for us. I firmly believe that boys need a man's strong guiding hand, to guide them into manly pursuits. Young boys need a strong hand at the helm.

Anderson: Come on Bob, you've got to be kidding. That kind of reasoning went out with black and white television.

Conrad: Enough, we need to get past this. Still, I wonder what this rule means for lesbians.

Baker: For who?

Anderson: Chris is right. This rule has devastating impacts on lesbians who come out after their divorce; the way the rule is written they will always be presumed to be the wrong parent with whom to place a male child.

Baker: This is ridiculous! I never heard of a mother being a lesbian. And even if they were mothers, well, I'd take their children away from them in a second. They're immoral.

Conrad: I hate to sound politically incorrect but sometimes I do think that modern social science supports this recommendation, even if it means we've ended up making the right recommendation purely by accident. And anyway, nobody ever thought that this rule had an impact on lesbians; the issue has simply never been on the table. We need to take a vote.

Anderson: Why take a vote now? Don't we usually discuss and then reconvene after we've had a chance to think about it?

Baker: Let's just do it. We know how we all feel.

Conrad: I agree with Bob.

WHEREUPON, a vote was taken and the motion to retain recommendation 5 and the accompanying comment was passed by a vote of 2-1, with Director Anderson in opposition.

EXHIBIT D

Memo to IFC Board of Directors

Memo

November 10, 2006

To: Board of Directors of the IFC
From: IFC Secretary and Archivist
Re: History of the Father-Male Child Preference

In response to the committee's request, I have researched the history of Recommendation 5.

Current IFC Recommendation 5 has been part of the IFC's Recommendations for Family Placement in Iowa Courts ever since those recommendations were first published in 1912. At that time the prevailing attitude was that, to quote the comment on the original recommendation,

> "The need for a man's guiding hand in raising a boy is unquestionable. Boys not receiving such guidance fall into femininity, dissoluteness and perversion, and fail to receive instruction in the manly arts, sports, and the need to respect the delicate flower that is young womanhood. The raising of a boy by only his mother, while sometimes unavoidable, is nevertheless contrary to nature and should be avoided whenever possible."

Recommendations on the Proper Judicial Placement of Orphans, Waifs and Children of Harlots (Des Moines, IFC Press, 1912), page 21.

Since then, Recommendation 5 has been more or less automatically incorporated into subsequent editions of the Recommendations. In 1975 the Board began a full-scale study and revision of all the recommendations; however, due to time and budget constraints, all that amounted from that effort was an updating of outdated language in the commentary to Recommendation 5, without any significant study of the underlying issue.

My research has not disclosed any express linkage between Recommendation 5 and concern for the sexual orientation of either the mother or the father. It is likely that for most of the period 1912-2006 it was simply assumed that homosexuals would not be parents, even though the official IFC commentary on several recommendations has included language that could be taken to manifest a disfavoring of homosexuals as parents. Much of this language has survived into the current version of the Recommendations.

CONSTITUTIONAL LAW
ESSAY EXAMINATION
ANSWERS

CONSTITUTIONAL LAW ESSAY EXAM #1

QUESTION #1

I. Adams v. Baker

1. Congressional Power to Enforce the Fourteenth Amendment   Baker could attempt to argue that Congress lacks the constitutional authority to enact the ORA. The most likely sources of such power are the Commerce Clause and §5 of the Fourteenth Amendment. Because §5, unlike the Commerce Clause, would allow Congress to authorize damages and back-pay awards, Seminole Tribe v. Florida (1996), that source will be analyzed first.

Congress has the power to "enforce" the Fourteenth Amendment. This allows Congress to enact laws that go beyond the liability rule announced by the Supreme Court, to remedy and prevent violations of that underlying rule (Boerne v. Flores (1997)). However, such statutes must be "congruent and proportional" to the underlying constitutional violation.

Is the ORA congruent and proportional? Probably not. The statute was most likely enacted to protect the equal protection rights of the obese; there is no fundamental right to employment that Congress might be seen as protecting. Obesity is not a suspect class; thus, such classifications get only rational basis scrutiny when challenged in court. This fact means that it will be harder for Congress to demonstrate a strong need for the legislation (Nevada v. Hibbs (2003)).

Here the evidence supporting the §5 basis for the ORA is weak. There is little evidence that states themselves are discriminating, and no evidence that any such state discrimination is actually unconstitutional. Although such weak evidence was accepted in Hibbs, in that case the challenged statute aimed at protecting the equality rights of women, which the Court has considered much more important, and thus which Congress has much more latitude to protect. Thus, the evidence in this case—public opinion evidence about the discomfort people feel about obese individuals, and a small amount of unexplained discrimination, only one instance of which was performed by a state—is probably insufficient.

It may be that the statute is weak enough that it could be supported by these weak evidentiary showings. But, with the rational-basis review given to obesity classifications and the weak evidence suggesting the seriousness of obesity discrimination, it's probably the case that the Court would accept only a statute that prohibited the type of obesity discrimination that a court itself would find to be unconstitutional. There is no evidence that the statute is that limited.

Conclusion: Probably no §5 basis for the statute.

2. Commerce Clause   The Court in U.S. v. Lopez (1995) said that Congress can regulate channels or instrumentalities of interstate commerce, or activities that substantially affect interstate commerce. Employment is not a channel or instrumentality of interstate commerce; thus, if the statute is a valid regulation of interstate commerce, it is because employment substantially affects interstate commerce.

In U.S. v. Morrison (2000) the Court said that, if the activity being regulated is economic, then the substantial effects inquiry could be done by aggregating individual instances of the activity being regulated, and that Congress would be deferred to in determining whether, in the aggregate, that activity substantially affected interstate commerce. Employment is clearly an economic activity unlike, in Lopez, school violence and, in Morrison, gender-based violence. Aggregating employment relationships, it is clear that they have a substantial effect on interstate commerce.

Conclusion: The ORA is probably a valid regulation of interstate commerce. But note that this does not mean that Congress may make states liable for retrospective relief such as damages or back pay (Seminole Tribe). Thus, Adams could not make such a claim against the State of Baker.

3. Regulation of a Traditional Government Function   In National League of Cities v. Usery (1976) the Court held that an otherwise valid Commerce regulation could not apply to a state's performance of a traditional government function. However, in Garcia v. San Antonio Transit Authority (1985), the Court overturned that result and allowed such regulation. Thus, there is no need to consider whether auditing is a traditional governmental function; to the extent the statute regulated the state as an employer, it is valid under the Commerce Clause.

4. Eleventh Amendment   Young relief: There is no problem with Adams's request for an injunction against the head auditor. Such a request is the kind of relief authorized by Ex parte Young (1908), as long as the relief is based on a federal, not a state, law violation, the suit is brought against a state official, not the state, and the injunction would not impair the state's sovereignty too much (Idaho v. Coeur d'Alene Tribe (1997)). All of these requirements are met here: the underlying law is federal, the request is aimed at the auditor, not the state itself, and an injunction against employment discrimination doesn't impact the state in the way that the requested relief did in Idaho, in which the plaintiff requested an injunction against the state official asserting sovereignty over certain territory claimed by the state.

II. CPOD v. Department of Labor

1. Standing   For an association to have standing it must satisfy the following three requirements:

- at least one member must have standing
- the topic of the lawsuit must be germane to the association's reason for existence
- the relief requested must work in the absence of a named individual member (United Food Workers v. Brown Group (1996))

a. Prong 1:   One member would almost surely have standing here. Standing requires injury, causation and redressability (Warth v. Seldin (1974)). If the regulation is too lenient, then most likely a fired person will be injured; at the very least, the person's job is less secure. The injury would be caused by the lenient regulation and the injury would be redressable by a court.

b. Prong 2:   Given what is said about the purpose of the organization, there's no question but that the suit would be germane to the organization's purpose of preventing discrimination against the obese.

c. Prong 3: Unlike damages, an injunction would benefit the individual members without any need for that member to be a formal part of the lawsuit. An injunction would prevent the regulation from taking effect, which would automatically benefit members.

2. Conclusion The Confederation would have standing.

III. Everett v. Fair Skies

1. Preemption The question is whether the ORA preempts state law, and, if not, whether the state law is nevertheless void under the Dormant Commerce Clause.

Preemption may be express or implied. Here, there is no express statement that Congress intended to preempt state law.

Is there implied preemption? Implied preemption may be based on conflict or field preemption.

Field preemption occurs when the federal regulatory scheme is so pervasive that it indicates a congressional intent to occupy the entire regulatory field. There is no indication that the ORA is so broad as to occupy the field of obesity discrimination; thus, field preemption is unlikely.

Conflict preemption may occur either when it is physically impossible to comply with both laws, or when compliance with the state law would frustrate federal objectives.

It's not physically impossible for an employer to comply with both laws; an employer could simply comply with the broader Illinois rule which would automatically comply with the federal rule.

It's possible, though, that the state law would conflict with federal objectives. The ORA seems to reflect a federal policy that some obesity discrimination may be appropriate, if it responds to consumer preferences. Compliance with the Illinois rule would force employers not to discriminate even though federal policy might not only allow, but also prefer, such discrimination. For that reason there is a chance a court would find the Illinois rule to be preempted.

2. Dormant Commerce Clause Assuming that the Illinois rule is not preempted it would be necessary to determine whether it violates the Dormant Commerce Clause. The rule is that if a state statute directly regulates interstate commerce it will almost assuredly be struck down (New Energy v. Limbaugh (1988)). If it discriminates against interstate commerce, the statute will be subjected to strict scrutiny, which will require that there be no less commerce-restrictive alternative to achieving the legitimate government interest sought to be furthered (Dean Milk v. Madison (1950). If it regulates interstate and in-state commerce evenhandedly, then it will be subject to a relatively deferential test under which the burdens on interstate commerce will be considered in light of the in-state benefits the statute provides (Minnesota v. Clover Leaf Creamery (1981)).

Here, the statute clearly is not discriminatory, as it is evenhanded both ostensibly and in application — all employers must comply, and there's no indication that out-of-state employers are especially burdened. Thus, under the deferential benefit-burden balancing test, the common law rule will probably survive, given the benefits it provides in-state in terms of equality of treatment.

Conclusion: If the Illinois rule is not preempted then it will probably survive, and Everett can bring her suit under that rule.

QUESTION #2

I. Anderson v. BigPharma

1. Standing   To have standing, Anderson has to show that he was

1. injured;
2. that the injury was caused by the defendant; and
3. that the injury could be redressable by a court (Warth v. Seldin (1974)).

The injury must be either currently existing or imminent, and must be particularized, i.e., must not be a generalized grievance (Lujan v. Defenders of Wildlife (1992)).

Injury: Anderson's injury to his professional practice is probably sufficient to satisfy this requirement. This case is unlike the standing theory rejected in Lujan. In that case, the researchers were not able to show that they were actually impacted by the statute; they had no plans to return to the areas where the endangered species lived. Here, Anderson alleges that he suffers injury to the practice of his profession as a result of the statute. Nor is this a generalized grievance; he suffers his own particular injury, even if other pharmacists might have their own similar injury.

Causation: Causation is probably satisfied too. This is not a case where the causal chain is extremely tight, as where the challenged action directly impacts the plaintiff. However, the link from the challenged action — the ad — to the injury is reasonable.

Redressability: Because fines or an injunction might deter the defendant from acting in this way in the future, and because damages might make Anderson whole, the injury is redressable by a court.

2. Free Speech/Commercial Speech   BigPharma would have a First Amendment defense to the statute. BigPharma's speech is commercial speech because it is speech that, presumably, proposes a commercial transaction. (It is possible that the speech could be considered noncommercial, if the advertisement talked about health in general, rather than promoting a particular product. This possibility is discussed below.) The test for commercial speech restrictions is set out in Central Hudson Gas v. Pub. Svc. Comm'n (1980).

To be protected at all the speech must be non-misleading and not related to unlawful activity. Here, the speech can be presumed to be not misleading, and not related to unlawful activity.

To be regulated, the government must have a substantial interest; the regulation must directly advance that interest; and a more limited restriction on speech will not serve that interest.

It can be asked whether the government's interest is substantial. This is not a question of government regulating for the health of consumers, because doctors still have to prescribe the drugs that consumers are requesting. Rather, there is simply concern with health-care costs rising because patients are demanding drugs that their doctors might not otherwise prescribe. Still, this is a fairly easy requirement to meet;

for example, in Central Hudson the Court accepted the state's interest in promoting energy conservation, given the energy shortage existing at the time. Even given how speech-protective the Supreme Court has read the Central Hudson test in recent years, this prong will most likely be held to have been satisfied.

The regulation clearly advances the interest in cost savings. It is perfectly reasonable to conclude that advertising will increase the demand for a product; here, advertising of drugs may increase consumer demand.

The statute may encounter problems under this prong. While the Court has not been consistent in how tight the "fit" has to be between the statute and the underlying goal, in recent years the Court has been more insistent on a tight fit, e.g., as in 44 Liquormart v. Rhode Island (1996). In particular, the Court may suggest that counter-advertising, advisements to doctors, or even restrictions on prescribing certain drugs might be less speech-restrictive means that would take care of the underlying problem.

II. Colorado v. HHS

1. Anti-Commandeering/Spending Power   On the face of the statute, it might seem like §2 unconstitutionally commandeers state governments, by requiring them to regulate the practice of medicine within their respective states. This would violate the rule in New York v. U.S. (1992), in which the Court held that the federal government could not require state legislatures to legislate on a particular topic.

However, the penalty for not acting in this case is the removal of federal funds. Congress has a great deal of latitude with regard to attaching conditions on federal funds (South Dakota v. Dole (1987)). As long as

1. the spending is in pursuit of the general welfare;
2. the condition is stated explicitly;
3. the condition is at least somewhat related to the spending grant; and
4. the condition doesn't violate another constitutional provision,

then the condition is constitutional. Here, Medicare spending clearly is in pursuit of the public interest, the condition is stated explicitly in the statute, it is related to Medicare spending (because general health care costs may affect Medicare costs). As far as the fourth requirement is concerned, there is a problem with §1 of the statute violating the First Amendment, but this particular section doesn't require the state to violate anyone's constitutional rights.

Conclusion: Colorado's challenge would fail.

QUESTION #3

I. Ned v. Ajax

1. State Action   The first question that has to be resolved is whether Ajax is a state actor. If it is not, then it is not required to abide by the Fourteenth Amendment.

The Court has found state action in four situations:

a. where the private party is performing a public function (Marsh v. Alabama (1946));

b. where the state is entangled with the private conduct (Burton v. Wilmington Parking Authority (1960));

c. where the legislature approves the private conduct (Reitman v. Mulkey (1967)); and

d. where courts enforce private discriminatory conduct (Shelley v. Kraemer (1948))

The last two of these possibilities can be excluded quickly; there's no explicit legislative approval of Ajax's action, nor is there judicial enforcement of private discriminatory conduct. Moreover, its doubtful that printing forms is the sort of traditional exclusively governmental conduct that a court would require before finding that the party was performing a public function. For example, it is very far from operating a company town, as in Marsh; rather, Ajax is simply providing an economic service that many private parties provide, both to government and to other private parties.

Thus, the only possibility for state action here is that there is entanglement. In cases such as Burton, however, the Court stressed not just whether the state was involved with the private firm, but also whether the state was involved with the particular conduct of the private firm that is the subject of the legal challenge (Jackson v. Metro Edison (1972)).

Here, there is no indication that the state is entangled with Ajax's personnel policies. Ajax is simply a supplier to the government, and even though it gets most of its business from the government that does not make it a state actor (Rendell–Baker v. Kohn (1982)). Because the state is not entangled with that aspect of Ajax's business, Ajax's conduct in this case will probably not be imputed to the state.

Conclusion: Probably no state action in this case.

2. Procedural Due Process Assuming the presence of state action, the first issue would be whether Ajax gave Ned an adequate hearing, consistent with due process. To make this claim, Ned would have to show:

a. that he had a liberty or property interest;

b. that was deprived; and

c. that he didn't get adequate process (Mathews v. Eldridge (1976))

a. Liberty or Property Interest? Ned probably had a property interest in his job. A property interest is created when government gives someone a reasonable expectation that he will continue to enjoy a benefit if he meets certain criteria (Roth v. Bd. of Regents (1972)). Even though he signed only year-to-year contracts, the tradition of long-time employment at Ajax plus the statement in the company manual would probably give him a reasonable expectation of continued employment, as long as he satisfied the criteria (which, of course, he wants a hearing to demonstrate). A similar situation arose in Perry v. Sinderman (1972) where such a statement and a long-term course of dealing was held to justify a hearing on whether a property interest existed.

b. Deprivation: A negligent action by the government may not deprive one of a property interest. However, in this case the deprivation was intentional, as the company acted purposefully in firing Ned.

c. Adequate Process: In Mathews the Court laid down a three-part balancing test to judge the adequacy of the procedure afforded an individual. The test balances:

1. the importance of the interest to the class of recipients;
2. the risk of error in the current procedures, and the possibility of improved accuracy if more procedure is provided; and
3. the government's interest

(1) Importance of the Interest: This factor will not weigh overly strongly in Ned's favor. Note that what he is losing here is his salary during the pendency of an oral hearing, which might take as long as six months. Although a salary is important, mid-level managers will probably be thought to have options that keep them from destitution should they be fired. Moreover, they may be presumed to have savings or other safety nets to cushion any shock. By contrast, in Goldberg v. Kelly (1970) the Court noted that welfare benefits, as designed for people who are otherwise destitute, were extremely important to that class.

(2) Risk of Error and Possibility of Improvement: The difference here is between a decision made on a paper record and one made after an oral hearing. Depending on the basis for the action, a paper record may or may not be prone to erroneous decisions, and an oral hearing may or may not increase accuracy. For example, in Goldberg the Court required an oral hearing, but in Mathews the Court did not. Mathews reasoned that the issue in that case — whether the claimant was disabled — could easily be made based on medical records, and that an oral hearing wouldn't add much accuracy, while noting that in Goldberg the Court was considering a decision to terminate welfare benefits, which turned on criteria that could be best determined through oral testimony.

In this case it's unclear what the criteria are. However, presumably employment reviews would account for most of the relevant criteria, because that's what they're designed to do. Thus, it's unclear whether an oral hearing would add much accuracy.

(3) Government's Interest: In this case the government's interest (again, assuming that Ajax "is" the government) would mainly be to avoid the expense of paying the salary during the pendency of the oral hearing. Moreover, if Ajax suspected Ned of malfeasance, it might be problematic for it to have him working, where he could potentially harm the company more — although this could be taken care of by suspending Ned on full pay.

Conclusion: On balance, these factors, especially 1 and 2, probably tip against Ned, and mean that he will lose his procedural due process claim.

3. *Discrimination*   Ned might be able to claim that he was the victim of racial discrimination. When government discriminates on the basis of race, the rule is strict scrutiny — the race-based action must be narrowly tailored to meet a compelling government interest (Palmore v. Sidoti (1984)). Here, it's highly unlikely that the government/Ajax could survive this, as there's no indication in the facts of any compelling reason to fire Ned on account of his race.

However, it's unclear whether Ajax fired Ned *because of* his race. This raises the question of intent. Governmental action, to run afoul of the Equal Protection Clause, must be intentionally discriminatory (Washington v. Davis (1976)). To establish intent, the following steps are taken:

1. Ned must start by proving that race was one of the reasons Ajax fired him.
2. If he shows this, then Ajax must prove that it would have taken the same action anyway, even in the absence of that intent.
3. If Ajax makes that showing, then the decision gets only rational basis review; if not, then the decisions would be race discrimination that would get strict scrutiny.

Here, there's no indication in the record that Ned was fired for racial reasons, although the facts are too sparse to be clear on this. Ned would have to make the showing explained above in order to shift the burden to Ajax, again as explained above.

CONSTITUTIONAL LAW ESSAY EXAM #2

QUESTION #1

I. County of Austin v. Baker

1. Obscenity   The general standard for judging the constitutionally protected status of sexual speech is the test from Miller v. California (1973). Miller requires that, for sexual speech to be unprotected, it must have the following characteristics:

  a. The material is such that, an average person, applying contemporary community standards, would say that, as a whole, it appeals to the prurient interest (prurience being lustful desire or lasciviousness);
  b. the material depicts or describes, in a patently offensive way, sexual conduct specifically defined by the applicable state law; and
  c. the material, taken as a whole, lacks serious literary, artistic, political, or scientific value.

The first and second prongs of this test are based on a community standard, but this is subject to a possible constitutional minimum (e.g., it would probably be constitutionally impermissible for any jury or judge to decide that, under a particular community's standard, the movie "Eyes Wide Shut" was patently offensive, see Jenkins v. Georgia (1974) (as a matter of law, "carnal knowledge" cannot be considered patently offensive)).

In addition, the Supreme Court has made it clear that child pornography using live child models is unprotected, even if it would otherwise be protected under Miller (Ferber v. New York (1982)).

These rules yield the following results:

  a. The child pornography would be subject to the Miller standard. It would not be subject the state's wider latitude to regulate child pornography, due to the lack of child models.
  b. The sex history books would probably be protected; even though they might show ultimate sex acts, these books would probably be held to have serious merit and thus be protected.
  c. The "Man's World" books would probably be protected. Incidental nudity alone is probably not enough to satisfy Miller, but even if it was a state could ban these books only as part of an overall ban on obscenity, or a ban on the "most obscene" books. But R.A.V. v. St. Paul (1992) and American Booksellers v. Hudnut (7th Cir. 1985) suggest that a state could not ban them based on their espousal of a particular viewpoint on, or their discussion of, the topic of gender relationships.
  d. The Sexart books might be unprotected. The fact that the acts depicted take place in front of reproductions of art doesn't therefore bestow artistic merit on the books. Because the books are designed only to titillate, there's a good chance that the first Miller prong is met; and because they depict ultimate

sex acts, if a state law defines those acts with particularity then there's a good chance that the second prong is satisfied. Without any more information about their merit, it seems like the third prong is also met, thus rendering the books susceptible to a government ban.

II. Alabama v. Collins

1. Incitement   The issue here is whether Collins can be prosecuted for her speech. The rule is provided by Brandenburg v. Ohio (1969), which states that, for speech to be subject to prosecution for inciting unlawful conduct, the speaker must have intended to incite such conduct as an immediate consequence of the speech (i.e., not at some indefinite later point) and that the speech have been objectively likely to succeed in doing so. The Court has generally been very speech protective in applying this test (e.g., Hess v. Indiana (1974); NAACP v. Claiborne Hardware (1982)).

     a. It's doubtful that the first prong is satisfied here. The speech was sharp, but its call for a "purge" seems far more metaphorical rather than a call to immediate action. Without more facts indicating that she intended immediate action — e.g., suggestions to that effect, or the brandishing of a weapon — it's doubtful that a court would find this prong satisfied.

     b. The second of these prongs is more difficult to analyze given the lack of facts about the emotional condition of the crowd. However, given how speech protective the Court has been in applying this test, it is likely that nothing short of an aroused crowd ready to act at a slight provocation by a speaker will satisfy this prong.

Conclusion: The prosecution will probably fail.

III. Baker v. The Divine Way

1. Libel   This issue raises the question of what standards the Constitution demands for libel convictions. Libel itself is not protected, but the First Amendment imposes restrictions on the standards of proof for libel claims to prevent speakers from being chilled from speaking due to a fear of large libel awards (New York Times v. Sullivan (1964)). The question turns on (1) the identify of the plaintiff as a public or a private figure, and (2) the nature of the question as one of public or private concern (Gertz v. Robert Welch (1974)). In general, public figure plaintiffs face a higher burden of proof, and claims of libel on matters of public interest also require higher standards.

In this case, Baker would probably be a private figure. Like the attorney in Gertz, there are no facts here to indicate that Baker sought the media out; he was simply a businessman engaging in his business. Nor is he a public official like the sheriff in Sullivan. However, the matter — the introduction of pornography into the community — is probably a matter of public concern, as it concerns the moral tone and character of the community. This can be compared to the situation in Dun & Bradstreet v. Greenmoss Builders (1985), which involved an allegedly libelous credit report sent by a credit-reporting agency to a requesting company, which the Court held to be concerning a purely private matter.

This is the same combination — private figure suing on a matter of public interest — at issue in Gertz. In that case, the Court stated that compensatory damages could be awarded if the plaintiff proved his case by any standard more than strict liability — in particular, negligence would be a constitutionally allowable standard for compensatory damages. However, punitive or presumed damages would have to be proven by a standard called "actual malice," which requires the plaintiff to prove that the defendant acted with either actual knowledge of the falseness of the statement, or reckless disregard of its falsity.

Here, Baker could surely prove negligence — the newsletter did not cross-check the information before it printed it, and it even got the name wrong of the person who had in fact been arrested. This might even suffice to show reckless disregard, because presumably any minimally careful editor would have noticed the different names and at least done some more investigation.

Conclusion: Baker can probably collect both compensatory and punitive damages.

QUESTION #2

I. Fair Marketing Act

1. Delegation of Legislative Power   There is probably not an unconstitutionally excessive delegation here. Under cases like Yakus v. United States (1944), as long as the power given to the agency is relatively limited, it doesn't matter that the ends are extremely broad. Here, the ends are fairly broad — to further public confidence in the economic system, and to ensure national prosperity. But the means the agency has to accomplish those ends are relatively limited: to promulgate regulations implementing the prohibition on misleading, unfair or unscrupulous telemarketing techniques. Just like in Yakus, in which Congress had fairly broad goals — to control price inflation during wartime — but gave the agency relatively narrow authority — to promulgate price controls consistent with several guidelines given in the statute — so too here the Congress sufficiently limits the agency's discretion so as to defeat a non-delegation claim. Compare this statute to that in Schechter Poultry v. United States (1935): in that case, Congress gave the agency nearly unlimited power (the power to promulgate codes of fair competition, with basically no standards governing what they were to include) to achieve an extremely broad goal (to improve the national economy). This statute is clearly more limited, both in its ends and especially in its means.

2. Impairment of the President's Enforcement Power   Again, this is probably not a problem. The job of drafting regulations to implement Congress' policy can easily be seen as executive in nature, but in Morrison v. Olson (1988) the Supreme Court allowed Congress to limit the President's authority to remove officers who execute federal law. The test in Morrison is whether the limitation is of such a nature as to impede the President's ability to perform his constitutional duty. Here, because the FFMA head is an inferior officer, who reports to another federal officer (the head of the FTC), there is less reason to expect that the Constitution requires the President to have complete control over the FFMA head's tenure. Also, the Court in Morrison concluded that the "good cause" provision gave the President sufficient control over the special prosecutor to allow the President to carry out his Constitutional duty; that same provision exists in this statute.

   3. Agency Adjudication   There is probably not a problem here. Under Schor v. Commodities Futures Trading Corp. (1986), the Court uses a multi-factor balancing test to determine whether an agency adjudication scheme unconstitutionally restricts the power of Article III courts. Those factors include:

   a. Is there significant Article III court review of the agency's decision? Here, the answer is yes; the standards of review are the same as those in Schor, which the Court found satisfactory.

   b. How much jurisdiction does the agency court have? Here, the agency court adjudicates only those issues arising out of unfair telemarketing claims. That is a limited jurisdiction that again would satisfy Schor.

   c. How much power does the agency court have? Here, the agency court does not have the power to enforce its own orders; again, this is significant under Schor's analysis.

   d. Is this a private or a public right? Because the right is created by government, it is closer to a public right than the right at issue in Schor. Under the statute, sometimes an individual may bring a claim against another individual; that sort of claim is a bit closer to a classic private right, as compared to a situation where the government is a party to the action, either as a plaintiff or defendant. But the private/public right issue is not dispositive; again, in Schor the right at issue was a classic private right — a common-law claim brought by one individual against another — and yet the Court allowed it to be heard in an agency court. Here too, then, a court would probably uphold the scheme.

   4. Legislative Veto?   There is a problem here with an unconstitutional legislative veto. This is a straightforward application of INS v. Chadha (1983). The act of Congress in overturning an agency regulation would be legislative in effect, as it would change the legal rights and duties of individuals (e.g., what would have been illegal under the regulation would not be so now). But Congress is attempting to achieve that legislative effect without presentment to the President. Thus, it is unconstitutional.

   5. Free Speech/Commercial Speech   The question is whether §2 violates the First Amendment, by prohibiting certain marketing speech.

   This is clearly commercial speech; indeed, it fits perfectly the definition of commercial speech as speech that proposes a commercial transaction (Virginia Bd. of Pharmacy v. Va. Consumer Council (1976)). Thus, the test from Central Hudson Gas v. Pub. Svc. Comm'n (1980) would apply:

   1. To be protected at all the speech must be non-misleading and not related to unlawful activity.

   To be regulated:

   2. the government must have a substantial interest;

   3. the regulation must directly advance that interest; and

   4. a more limited restriction on speech will not serve that interest.

Here, it is quite easy to stop at prong one, because the statute explicitly regulates only offers conveyed in a "misleading or fraudulent manner." There is no need to go on with the rest of the analysis, as the speech is without protection.

If one were to go on with the analysis, then the court would surely find that government has a substantial interest in preventing fraud, that penalizing misleading speech directly serves that purpose, and that the restriction is narrowly tailored. Indeed, because fraud is itself a crime, there would be no question, as there was in 44 Liquormart v. Rhode Island (1996), that government could take the less speech-restrictive step of regulating the underlying activity — the activity itself here (fraud) is the speech, and there is no question but that government has the constitutional power to penalize fraud.

QUESTION #3

I. U.S. v. Billy Zoom

1. Free Speech/Time, Place, and Manner Restrictions   Billy can argue that the curfew violated his speech rights. The proper analysis here is whether the curfew is a legitimate time, place, or manner (TPM) restriction. The TPM test asks:

1. Is the restriction content-neutral?
2. Is it narrowly tailored to further a significant government interest?
3. Does it leave open ample alternative means of communication?

Clearly the restriction is content-neutral, at least on its face. While it might be argued that the only people protesting are the anti-World Trade Organization (WTO) demonstrators, the fact that the law has been on the books for years indicates that it was not intended to burden speech about the WTO in particular. While it might be debated how important it is to ensure a good night's sleep for hotel guests, guarding against the possibility of drunken confrontations surely would rank as a significant government interest. In terms of narrow tailoring, remember that the TPM test, as interpreted in cases like Ward v. Rock Against Racism (1989), is quite deferential; that is, once the restriction is not suspected of being aimed at particular content, the Court allows the government a great deal of latitude in solving the problems caused by protests and other speech. Here, a court would probably defer to the City's judgment that this was an appropriate step to take, as long as the restriction didn't completely shut off the protesters' speech (which it doesn't here, since they can make their points during the daytime).

2. Free Speech/Symbolic Speech   The passport-burning charge obviously implicates the symbolic speech doctrine. It is not speech per se that is being restricted (as in the above discussion), but instead conduct that has an expressive component. In evaluating the constitutionality of such conduct restrictions that have speech implications, the Court asks:

1. If the government has the constitutional power to take the action;
2. If the restriction was motivated by a desire to suppress expression; and
3. If the restriction was narrowly tailored to serve a significant government interest.

Clearly it is within the power of the federal government to criminalize the destruction of passports, as part of Congress' power over immigration. Presumably that restriction was not motivated by a desire to suppress expression, although if you had legislative history that Congress had in fact been concerned with, say, anti-Vietnam war or pro-Communist demonstrations where people burned their passports, then there might be an argument that this requirement was not satisfied. As with TPM restrictions, once it is clear that the government is not targeting expression, the Court becomes more deferential, allowing the government latitude to determine the best way to further its non-speech related interests (see, for example, the application of the test in Clark v. Center for Creative Non-Violence (1984)).

Conclusion: Billy would probably lose both of his First Amendment arguments.

II. Carl v. City of Seattle

1. Contracts Clause   Carl might attempt to argue that the action violated the Contracts Clause, by impairing the obligations of his contract with the theater troop. Clearly, there is a contractual obligation which has been impaired—the order stated that the relevant contracts were "null and void."

The Contracts Clause does not prohibit any impairment of contracts, because much government action impairs contractual rights in one way or another. Thus, the general rule has developed that only substantial impairments will be scrutinized (Allied Structural Steel v. Spannus (1976)). If the impairment is deemed substantial, then it will be scrutinized more carefully the greater the impairment.

In determining whether and how substantial the impairment is, the Court will generally look at the raw degree of impairment, as well as the extent to which the government action upsets the parties' reasonable expectations. Once the substantiality of the impairment is determined, the Court will then balance that impairment against the state's interest.

Applying this test is highly fact-specific. Here, we don't know how large the contract was, and how big a part of Carl's business it represents. Moreover, because this is a seemingly temporary measure, it may not be as severe an impairment as in cases in which the Court has found unconstitutional impairment. In Allied, for example, the state changed an employer's contractual obligations with its employees relating to its pension obligations; those obligations are long-term funding commitments. By contrast, the impairment here affected a one-time sale; indeed, had the contract called for delivery at some future point, it would not even have been impaired at all. Thus, there is a good argument that the impairment is not substantial, or, if it is, it is justified by the government's need to prevent toy guns and handcuffs from causing problems for the police during a period of civil disturbance.

Conclusion: Carl will probably lose his Contracts Clause claim.

Note also that Carl does NOT have a substantive due process right to contract claim. Substantive due process protects the right to contract going forward—i.e., the right to form contracts. The claim here is that the government action impaired an existing contract.

III. State v. Dana

1. Free Speech/Fighting Words   Dana could argue that his speech was protected by the First Amendment. Fighting words are not protected speech (Chaplinsky v. New Hampshire (1942)). In defense to the incitement claim, however, he could try to claim that the Constitution protects speech like this, under Cohen v. California (1971). In that case the Court threw out a claim of disorderly conduct because there was no evidence that the defendant was threatening a particular person, and no evidence that any particular person was close to being goaded into physical violence. Here, however, the protesters made eye contact with individual workers, and it seems at least reasonable that the kind of words that were said, in the context (shouted, outside the gate of the plant that was the subject of the protest) might be enough to distinguish the speech here from Cohen.

Conclusion: There is a chance Dana could be convicted.

CONSTITUTIONAL LAW ESSAY EXAM #3

QUESTION #1

I. Peter v. Stallone

1. Interstate Commerce Power Commerce Clause: Cruelty to one's pets is a non-economic activity, therefore the deferential analysis of United States v. Darby (1941) and similar cases doesn't apply. Under United States v. Lopez (1995) a statute might benefit either from a jurisdictional nexus or from congressional fact-findings revealing an interstate commerce tie to the regulated activity. Here, there's no jurisdictional nexus, and the fact-finding probably doesn't help because the analysis that fact-finding supports is the attenuated sort disapproved in United States v. Morrison (2000). Thus, the statute is probably invalid under the Commerce Clause.

2. Commandeering The statute also commandeers state law-enforcement apparatus, especially by requiring that complaints be investigated "promptly." The state has no choice here, so it's not an example of "cooperative federalism," in which the federal government gives the state a chance to implement federal policy, but is not forced to. Thus, the statute runs afoul of United States v. Printz (1997), which extended the anti-commandeering rule of New York v. United States (1992) to law enforcement.

There is no commandeering problem, however, with the statute's requirement that state courts hear claims against private parties. In Printz the Court distinguished Testa v. Katt (1947), which had allowed Congress to make federal law causes of action hearable in state courts. The Court also explained that such a requirement did not commandeer state courts, because those courts were required to adjudicate claims based on applicable law, and federal law is supreme over state law by virtue of the Supremacy Clause of Article VI. Therefore, there is no problem with commandeering state courts, as there is with commandeering state legislatures or state law enforcement.

II. Peter v. Park Police

1. Regulation of Traditional State Government Functions There might have been a problem enforcing this statute against the state, based on the rule in National League of Cities v. Usery (1976), that an Article I-based law could not regulate how the state provides a traditional government function. But National League was overruled by Garcia v. San Antonio Transit Authority (1985), which allowed this sort of regulation, on the theory that states enjoyed protections from inappropriate federal regulation through the political process. Thus, this particular objection to the statute is invalid.

2. State Sovereign Immunity/Eleventh Amendment Enforcement of the statute raises problems with regard to state sovereign immunity. Here there is a clear statement of Congress' intent to abrogate state sovereign immunity. But Article I doesn't allow Congress to make states suable in state court (Alden v. Maine (1999)). What about Ex parte Young (1908)? Remember from Alden that all the Eleventh Amendment rules about Young apply now to state courts. You could conceivably sue the head of the state police (Young), for an injunction (allowed under Edeleman v. Jordan (1974)), under the federal law, because Pennhurst Hospital v. Halderman (1985) doesn't allow suits against states based on state law violations.

Under Idaho v. Coeur d'Alene Tribe (1997) the Court requires that the Court requires that Young relief not affect the state too heavily in its sovereign capacity. But in this case that argument would be doubtful. The Court in Idaho was faced with a situation in which the plaintiff sought an injunction preventing state officers from exercising the state's jurisdiction over particular lands, relief the Court found to implicate the state's sovereign interest. Here, by contrast, the intrusion on state sovereignty is much less.

However, there is a sovereign immunity problem because the statute seems to include a detailed remedial scheme. Under Seminole Tribe v. Florida (1996), such schemes make Young relief unavailable, on the theory that, by prescribing the detailed remedial scheme in the statute, Congress has impliedly precluded Young relief. Here, the relief seems detailed, prescribing the precise relief available for various numbers of infractions. Thus, Young relief might not be available.

QUESTION #2

I. Anderson Plating v. California

The question raises issues of Congress' ability to enact the federal law, and, assuming it has that power, the remaining vitality of the California law.

1. Interstate Commerce Power   Congress' power here turns on the Interstate Commerce Clause. There is no spending or taxing going on, and no other federal regulatory power, such as the immigration and naturalization power, and no serious argument that civil rights are being enforced.

In United States v. Lopez (1995) the Court set forth three categories of valid interstate commerce regulation:

1. regulation of the channels of interstate commerce;
2. regulation of the instrumentalities of interstate commerce; and
3. regulation of intrastate activities that substantially affect interstate commerce.

The Court in Lopez and United States v. Morrison (2000) also stated that, with regard to the third category, the constitutionality of regulation of economic activity will be reviewed more deferentially by the Court than regulation of non-economic activity. In particular, with regard to economic activity the Court will give more deference to legislative judgments that the local activity substantially affects interstate commerce, and will also be willing to make the substantial effects determination based on the aggregation of all the transactions regulated by the challenged statute.

Here, the statute will most likely be reviewed as a regulation of intrastate activities that affect interstate commerce. Of course, transportation activities also emit greenhouse gases, but the statute is not limited to such activities. Instead, the statute catches all greenhouse emitting activities, which probably means that it will be analyzed under the third Lopez category.

Within that category, it's probably the case that the statute regulates economic activity. Emission of greenhouse gases is normally a by-product of manufacturing or transportation or agriculture, all activities the Court would consider economic, as it did in Lopez when it distinguished Wickard v. Fillburn (1942), which dealt with agriculture, on that basis. Given this fact, the Court will probably be relatively deferential to congressional power, allowing Congress the benefit of the doubt on its implicit conclusion that such activities, in the aggregate, substantially affect interstate commerce.

Conclusion: The statute is probably within Congress' regulatory power.

2. Preemption   Having determined that the statute is probably within Congress' regulatory power, it then becomes necessary to consider the validity of the California statute. First, it is necessary to consider whether the state law is preempted by the federal statute. Assuming it is not, it then becomes necessary to see whether the state law falls as a violation of the Dormant Commerce Clause.

Preemption seeks to determine whether Congress intended to displace state law. A valid federal statute may do this, given the Supremacy Clause of Article VI, but only if Congress manifests the intent to do so. The Court finds this intent either through an express congressional statement or impliedly. Because there is no express statement in the statute, the question then becomes whether the federal law impliedly preempts the state law.

Implied preemption can be based on conflict or field preemption concerns. In field preemption, the court concludes that Congress intended the federal law to occupy the entire regulatory field, free of state law on the same subject. Usually this occurs when the federal law is so comprehensive as to convince a court that Congress intended to occupy the field.

Conflict preemption occurs either when it is physically impossible to comply with both the federal and state law, making the state law necessarily invalid, or when the state law, although not literally incompatible with federal law, nevertheless interferes with federal regulatory policy.

Finally, throughout the preemption inquiry there is normally a presumption against preemption; that is, a court will presume there is no preemption unless it is convinced otherwise. This presumption does not apply where the subject of the legislation is one traditionally subject to federal, rather than state, power.

In this case, there is no indication that Congress intended to occupy the field of greenhouse gas emissions. Indeed, the presumption would apply here, because environmental regulation is a traditional state concern. Given that presumption, and given that there is nothing in the federal statute that seems completely to occupy the field, this form of preemption probably doesn't apply.

Is there physical impossibility/conflict preemption here? No, because it is quite easy to comply both with the federal and the state laws. All one has to do is stop emitting these gases, and one has complied with both federal and the state law.

However, there may be federal policy impairment preemption. The federal statute makes it clear that it wants both to minimize the output of greenhouse gases while also maintaining economic prosperity. This is evident from the congressional findings, as well as from the cautious tone of the statute's prohibition, and its mandate to NOAA to study the issue more. Compliance with California's more draconian law may well frustrate this federal objective by leading to the phasing out of more emissions than federal policy makers would have preferred at this time. For that reason, the federal policy of balancing environmental protection and economic growth seems in danger from California's policy. Even given the presumption against preemption, this seems like a strong argument for preemption.

Conclusion: The California law is probably preempted, and thus invalid.

3. Dormant Commerce Clause   Assuming that the state law is not preempted, one would have to do a Dormant Commerce Clause analysis. The Dormant Commerce Clause imposes a near-absolute ban on direct state regulation of interstate commerce, a strict scrutiny review of state laws that discriminate against interstate commerce, and a deferential balancing test for state laws that regulate local and interstate commerce evenhandedly.

Here, the California law seems to regulate local and interstate commerce evenhandedly; any emissions production in California is subject to the limit. Nor is there any indication that the statute, even though seemingly evenhanded, works to the benefit of local industry at the expense of out-of-state commerce (compare Hunt v. Washington Apple Producers (1976)). Thus, the benefit/burden balancing test from Minnesota v. Clover Leaf Creamery (1981) will probably be used. That test measures the burdens the statute places on interstate commerce against the local benefits it provides, with the test skewed in favor of the validity of the state law. Here, California can argue that the statute provides local benefits by reducing greenhouse emissions (even if the benefit of that reduction is spread around the world) while imposing no particular burdens on interstate, as opposed to local, commerce. If the state law were so draconian as to shut down all industry in California in exchange for only a minor environmental benefit, that might present a different story. But the facts don't suggest such an extreme lack of balance. Thus, if the state law were not preempted, it would probably survive under the Dormant Commerce Clause.

Conclusion: The California law would probably survive Dormant Commerce Clause scrutiny.

QUESTION #3

I. Mary Hartman v. State of California and Director of Cal-Ag

1. State Sovereign Immunity/Eleventh Amendment   This question raises an issue of state sovereign immunity. The Eleventh Amendment imposes limits on the ability of individuals to sue non-consenting states. In particular, it prevents Congress from making states liable for retrospective relief when Congress legislates pursuant to its Article I powers (Seminole Tribe v. Florida (1996)). It also prevents federal courts from hearing state law causes of action against non-consenting states (Pennhurst Hospital v. Halderman (1985)). However, to ensure the supremacy of federal law, individuals may sue state officials (not states themselves) for injunctive relief (Ex parte Young (1908)). These same rules apply to suits against states in state court, under the Tenth Amendment (Alden v. Maine (1999)). In this case Mary's suit is based on federal law, as she is alleging that the state regulation failed to satisfy the requirements of the federal statute.

Given these rules, it is clear that Mary's claim for damages cannot go forward in federal or state court, under Seminole Tribe and Alden. However, she should be able to continue in her suit against the Director of Cal-Ag for the injunctive relief she seeks. She should be able to pursue that suit in either federal or state court. There is no objection to her bringing suit in state court, under the anti-commandeering rule of New York v. United States (1992) or Printz v. United States (1997), because the Supreme Court has made it clear that Congress may authorize federal law-based suits in state court. In Printz the Court made this clear, reaffirming its holding to that effect in Testa v. Katt (1947).

There might be two limitations on a Young suit relevant here. The first would be if §5 of the statute is understood to include a "detailed remedial scheme." Under Seminole Tribe, if Congress includes such a scheme, that action will be taken as an implicit preclusion of Young-type relief, thus making that relief unavailable. In this case, though, the relief authorized in §5 is quite broad, unlike the intricate set of remedies prescribed in the statute at issue in Seminole Tribe. Therefore, §5 should not be taken as precluding relief.

The second limitation might be if the injunctive relief Mary sought — to force the agency to promulgate tougher regulations — was thought to impact the state's sovereign interests too heavily. This was the problem in Idaho v. Coeur d'Alene Tribe (1997), in which the plaintiffs sought an injunction against state officials exercising jurisdiction over certain land. The Supreme Court in that case held that that relief impacted the state in its role as sovereign, and thus was not allowable under Young. Here, the relief sought does impact the state as a sovereign to some degree. But any Young relief impacts the state in some way. Depending on how aggressively a court reads Idaho, this might or might not be a problem here.

Conclusion: Mary should be able to sue in federal or state court, but only the Director of Cal-Ag, and only for injunctive relief, and only if the court decides that such relief would not violate Idaho.

II. AAPP v. U.S. Dept. of Agriculture

1. Ripeness This question raises an issue of ripeness, which is one of the justiciability doctrines the Supreme Court has found implicit in Article III's limitation of the federal judicial power to "cases or controversies." In Abbott Labs v. Gardner (1967), the Court stated the modern rule for ripeness, which it described as a test that balanced

> a. the fitness of the issue for judicial review; and
> b. the hardship to the parties of delaying judicial action.

In Abbott Labs the Court found that the nature of the issue as purely one of the agency's statutory authority to act as it did rendered the issue fit for judicial review; that is, further factual development would not have assisted the court in deciding the case. Here, the claims that AAPP have relate to the constitutionality of the statute. Those claims probably present pure legal questions whose resolution would not be affected by further factual development. Thus, the first Abbott Labs prong cuts in favor of review now.

With regard to the second prong, dealing with the hardship to the parties, the matter is less clear. Because the statute is so vaguely written, and because it provides that each state shall provide its own set of regulations for duck raising, it will not be clear what sorts of hardships will be placed on duck producers until the states present their regulations to the federal agency and that agency decides whether to accept them. Thus, this prong may cut against ripeness, unlike in Abbott Labs, in which the regulations would have forced the plaintiffs in that case either to destroy valuable stocks of advertising materials or run the risk of being cited as selling adulterated drugs. That difficult choice is not presented to the duck producers in this case.

On balance it's therefore unclear how a court would rule on the ripeness issue. Ultimately, though, because the issue is presented cleanly to the court, without a need for further factual development, a court might decide that it makes sense to hear the challenge now, since it has already been brought.

Conclusion: Although the issue is not clear, a court might well decide that the issue is ripe.

2. Interstate Commerce Power   The AAPP would be able to argue that the statute violates the Interstate Commerce power.

In United States v. Lopez (1995) the Court set forth three categories of valid interstate commerce regulation:

1. regulation of the channels of interstate commerce;
2. regulation of the instrumentalities of interstate commerce; and
3. regulation of intrastate activities that substantially affect interstate commerce.

Here, the statute does not regulate channels or instrumentalities of interstate commerce; thus, if it is to be valid, it must be as a regulation of an activity that substantially affects interstate commerce. In general, if an activity is economic, the Court will be more deferential to a congressional determination that the activity substantially affects interstate commerce (Lopez), and will allow a finding of substantial effects to be based on an aggregation of the effects of individual transactions regulated by the statute.

Here, the activity at issue will probably be considered economic. Duck production, like the raising of wheat in Wickard v. Fillburn (1942), is an economic activity. Some duck raisers may raise ducks only for their own personal consumption. Still, the Court in Lopez nevertheless classified the analogous situation in Wickard, in which the farmer was raising wheat in part for his own consumption, as economic. Thus, the deferential approach set forth above will be applied, and most likely the activity will be considered to substantially affect interstate commerce.

Conclusion: The statute is probably a valid regulation of interstate commerce.

3. Commandeering   The AAPP would be able to argue that the statute commandeers state government. In New York v. United States (1992), the Supreme Court held that a statute that commanded a state to engage in regulation of a given area violated the Tenth Amendment, by forcing a state government to consider regulation it may not have decided to consider on its own. In Printz v. United States (1997), the Court expanded this rule to prohibit federal commandeering of state law enforcement.

Here, the statute requires state government to designate an agency of the state responsible for duck safety, and for that agency to promulgate regulations on this issue. It is true that neither New York nor Printz dealt with state commandeering of a state's administrative apparatus; however, some executive action is required in the designation of the appropriate agency to deal with the issue, and, ultimately, administrative action is analogous to law enforcement. Thus, there is at least some argument that the statute runs afoul of the anti-commandeering rule.

Conclusion: The statute might violate the anti-commandeering rule.

CONSTITUTIONAL LAW ESSAY EXAM #4

QUESTION #1

I. CBC v. Retirement World

1. State Action   The first question that has to be asked is whether Retirement World is a state actor at all. Only a state government and its sub-entities are bound by the Fourteenth Amendment, not private parties. In determining whether an ostensibly private party is in fact acting in a way that requires adherence to constitutional requirements, the courts have found four categories of state action:

    a. private parties performing public functions;

    b. government entangled with private parties;

    c. legislative approval of private action; and

    d. judicial enforcement of private action.

Here, the only possible category that fits is the first one. In Marsh v. Alabama (1946) the Court found a company-owned town to be a state actor, as it had all the features of a town. The facts here are quite similar to that in Marsh, except that the residents themselves own the town. Homeowners of course are not state actors, but when they act together to create the semblance of a town, there is much more reason to find state action. While shopping centers have been found not to be state actors (Hudgens v. NLRB (1976)), the facts here are much closer to Marsh. Thus, even though the public function prong of the state action doctrine is limited, this is probably one situation where it would apply.

Conclusion: Retirement World is probably a state actor.

2. Free Exercise Clause   The question is whether the first ordinance violates the Free Religious Exercise Clause of the First Amendment. Generally speaking, if a statute burdens religious conduct only incidentally, as part of a generally applicable rule of conduct, then the Free Exercise claim fails (Employment Division v. Smith (1990)). In Smith, for example, a generally applicable rule that firing from a job for drug use disqualifies one for unemployment compensation was held valid, despite the fact that it burdened the religious exercise of the plaintiffs, who smoked a hallucinogenic drug as part of a Native American religious ritual. However, government action aimed at religious exercise in particular will be subject to strict scrutiny and probably struck down (Church of the Babalu Aye v. Hialeah (1993)).

Here, there is reason to suspect that the statute, even though facially neutral, was motivated by concerns over the CBC's rituals. The impetus from the statute arose because of the discovery of the cult's action, and its exceptions suggest that very little animal cutting will be banned except that done by the CBC. Note also that any legitimate interest the town might have had in protecting animals could have been taken care of by an animal theft and/or an animal cruelty statute that would not have been so closely targeted at the CBC's actions.

Note finally that it doesn't matter whether the ritual is central or peripheral to the religion's dogma. The Supreme Court has been unwilling to inquire, in Free Exercise cases, into the centrality of a particular ritual.

Conclusion: The cutting ordinance is probably unconstitutional.

3. Free Speech/Time, Place, and Manner Regulation   The parade ordinance seems to be a targeted law masquerading as a neutral law, here, a time, place, and manner restriction on speech. The first requirement of such restrictions is that they be content-neutral. Here, the ordinance is facially neutral, but because it was enacted immediately after the CBC started requesting permits, and because its numerical cutoff is just under the number of people necessary for the ritual, there's good reason to believe that it is content-based. Thus, as a content-based restriction on speech in a traditional public forum—a street—the ordinance would have to satisfy strict scrutiny.

It is unlikely that the statute could satisfy strict scrutiny. There is no compelling reason for the restriction, except residents' dislike of the speech or their fear that it will lead to converts, neither of which is a legitimate, let alone a compelling, reason for restricting speech.

If for some reason a court held that the ordinance was in fact content-neutral, then the ordinance would have to be narrowly tailored and allow the speakers an alternative means of making their message heard (Ward v. Rock Against Racism (1989)). The narrow tailoring requirement here is not as strict as the similarly worded requirement in equal protection (Ward). Even so, it might be asked whether the speakers did in fact have an alternative means of speaking, because the ordinance bans all marches of six or more people for six months, thereby making it impossible for the CBC to perform the ritual as it is required to be performed, i.e., with seven individuals. Moreover, the ban on use of props would also make the ritual harder to perform, and thus burden speech, probably unnecessarily (since any legitimate government interest, such as a concern for safety or litter, could be taken care of by less speech restrictive means). A total ban on marches for that long a period is a significant burden on speech, which might fail even the lenient time, place, or manner test.

Under either analysis, then, the ordinance is probably unconstitutional.

Conclusion: The parade ordinance would probably be declared unconstitutional.

QUESTION #2

I. AAA v. North Dakota

1. Standing   This question raises the question of when associations can sue. In Warth v. Seldin (1974) the Court set out the requirements an association would have to meet before it could sue on behalf of its members:

1. An individual member would have to have standing;
2. The subject of the lawsuit would have to be germane to the association's reason for existing; and
3. The relief would have to work in the absence of the individual member.

Here, an individual member such as Al would probably have standing to sue. The individual would be injured by the law, as it would allow smoking inside state buildings, to the detriment of a member's health. The injury would be caused by the defendant, because the law allowed that smoking to take place, and an injunction against the law would remedy the injury.

Here, the association was determined by Congress to be concerned with this sort of issue. Under United Food Workers v. Brown Group (1996), a congressional statement to this effect satisfies this prong of the associational standing test.

Finally, an injunction against the statute would remedy the member's injury, without the member having to be a named party. In general, injunctions are appropriate relief for associations seeking to sue on behalf of their members, while damages are not, because there would be no assurance that the money would flow to the member himself.

2. Commandeering of State Courts/Article III The statute authorizes suit in federal and state court. There is no problem with either authorization. With regard to federal courts, Article III allows Congress to place within federal court jurisdiction cases arising under federal law, such as the federal statute in this case. With regard to state courts, the Supreme Court stated in Testa v. Katt (1947) that Congress could require appropriate state courts to hear federal law causes of action.

3. State Sovereign Immunity/Eleventh Amendment If the federal statute is valid, it is because it is within Congress' authority under the Interstate Commerce Clause. Under Seminole Tribe v. Florida (1996), neither the Commerce Clause nor any other Article I power authorizes Congress to make states liable for retrospective relief, such as damages, due to the Eleventh Amendment. Thus, such relief would not be available. Here, the remedial scheme Congress enacted would be a violation of the Seminole Tribe rule, because it includes such retrospective relief as a major component.

Normally, plaintiffs can seek relief from the state by suing a state official and seeking prospective relief, such as damages (Ex parte Young (1908)). However, in Seminole Tribe the Court held that such relief would not available if Congress had inserted a detailed remedial scheme into the statute, on the theory that by doing so, Congress had impliedly precluded Young relief. Thus, even though that remedial scheme is itself invalid, the fact that Congress passed it reflects Congress' intent to preclude Young relief. Thus, Young relief would not be available.

4. Interstate Commerce Power The question is whether this statute is a valid regulation of interstate commerce. In United States v. Lopez (1995) the Court set forth three categories of valid interstate commerce regulation:

1. regulation of the channels of interstate commerce;
2. regulation of the instrumentalities of interstate commerce; and
3. regulation of intrastate activities that substantially affect interstate commerce.

Here, the statute does not regulate channels or instrumentalities of interstate commerce; thus, if it is to be valid, it must be as a regulation of an activity that substantially affects interstate commerce. In general, if an activity is economic, the Court will be more deferential to a congressional determination that the activity substantially affects interstate commerce (Lopez), and will allow a finding of substantial effects to be based on an aggregation of the effects of individual transactions regulated by the statute.

Here, the statute does not seem to regulate an economic activity per se. Smoking is not just regulated in buildings where economic activity is taking place, but also in places such as schools, churches, and other locations where non-economic activity goes on.

The Court is much less deferential when non-economic activity is regulated. The Court has suggested that either a jurisdictional nexus or fact-findings indicating the tie-in between the activity and interstate commerce might be useful. However, United States v. Morrison (2000) criticized fact-findings of the type that tied the regulated activity to interstate commerce simply by noting the eventual economic impact of the activity. Thus, in Morrison the Court criticized the finding that gender-motivated violence affected commerce by dissuading women from traveling and increasing insurance costs. In this statute, the fact-finding is similar, as Congress notes the insurance costs caused by health claims arising from smoking.

Without other relevant fact-findings, and without a jurisdictional nexus (i.e., a requirement that prosecutions under the statute show that the particular application of the statute directly impacted interstate commerce, for example, because the public location was an airport), the Court would probably find the statute to fail the test.

5. Regulation of Traditional State Governmental Function Note that there is no special problem in making the statute applicable to North Dakota government. Under National League of Cities v. Usery (1976) the Court would have inquired whether an otherwise-valid commerce regulation was invalid because it regulated how a state provided a traditional governmental function. However, in Garcia v. San Antonio Transit Authority (1985), the Court overruled National League. The current rule is that generally applicable economic regulation may be imposed on states. Note, however, that this conclusion does not obviate problems that might arise when a plaintiff attempts to vindicate that right by suing a state. As noted earlier, that issue implicates the Eleventh Amendment, which limits the amenability of states to lawsuits alleging violations of federal law.

QUESTION #3

I. Anderson and Acton v. CMA

1. State Action First, there is a question whether the CMA is a state actor. A private party can be called a state actor if it performs a public function, if the government is entangled with particular action done by the private party, or if the legislature approves or the courts enforce the private conduct.

Here, the state has delegated "sovereign power" to the CMA, which strongly suggests that the CMA is performing a public function. It may also be that the state would be considered to have entangled itself with the CMA, because California expressly authorizes the CMA to develop ethical standards for medical practice — the very standards that are challenged in this case.

Conclusion: Probably state action here.

2. Substantive Due Process   Assuming the CMA's action is attributable to the state, the next question is whether it deprives A and A of liberty without due process. The Court has recognized that the liberty protected by due process has a substantive component, and goes beyond the explicit provisions of the Bill of Rights that are incorporated against the states (Roe v. Wade (1973)). In general, if a state action infringes on a fundamental right, then the court will apply strict scrutiny to that action. If not, then it will apply the rational basis standard.

Thus, it becomes necessary to identify the interest. The problem is that the Court is not settled on how specifically or generally to identify the interest. Thus, it's not clear whether it would identify the interest as A and A's right, as a same-sex couple, to have a child by cloning, or more generally the right of people to become parents. See, e.g., Michael H. v. Gerald D. (1989) for an example of this disagreement.

If a court characterized the interest narrowly, it would probably find the interest not to be fundamental, as it is not deeply rooted in American history and tradition. In that case, it would apply the rational basis standard, which simply asked if the action is rationally related to a legitimate government interest. Here, the ban on cloning would rationally be related to the legitimate interest of preventing an untried and risky medical procedure that might lead people, at least, to experience emotional distress.

If the court characterized the issue more generally, as the right to be a parent, the issue would be closer. Government would need to show that the action was narrowly tailored to meet a compelling government interest. It might be able to do this; given the seriousness of harms that might arise from cloning, it might be that only a ban would take care of the problem. But this still might be overbroad, and a court might find that the ultimate decision whether to clone should remain with the individual, with the state only able to inform the choice by restricting it or requiring the individual to take steps (e.g., counseling) before undertaking the process.

Conclusion: Uncertain how this claim might be resolved.

3. Equal Protection   A and A might be able to argue that the ethical canon violates the Equal Protection Clause by discriminating against gays and by making it harder for them to have children (because heterosexuals can have them through childbirth). The Supreme Court has never held sexual orientation to be a suspect class, but in Romer v. Evans (1996) it did strike down a statute as unconstitutionally discriminating against gays.

However, before reaching that issue the Court would have to decide whether the statute actually classifies on the basis of gays. Discriminatory impact does not equal discrimination under the Equal Protection Clause; discriminatory intent is required (Washington v. Davis (1976)).

i. Discriminatory Intent: In order to determine whether the canon discriminates, the court would perform a burden-shifting analysis:

1. The plaintiff has to prove that the government action was motivated in part by an intent to discriminate;
2. If he makes that showing then the government must prove that, even absent that discriminatory intent it would have made the same decision. If

it proves that, then the court simply does rational basis review; otherwise, it considers the action discrimination against that group and applies the appropriate level of scrutiny.

Discrimination can be shown by a variety of sources, including legislative history, a history of previous discrimination, foreseeability of the discriminatory impact, and substantive or procedural deviations from normal government decision-making (Metro. Housing Corp. v. Village of Arlington Hts. (1977)).

Here, the evidence from the minutes suggests no explicit intent to discriminate; instead, the board seems motivated by neutral concerns about cloning. However, they are aware that the canon will harm gay people especially, and there is some procedural irregularity in the canon adoption process.

Nevertheless, it's probably the case that, even if A and A could carry their burden of showing at least some discriminatory intent, the CMA could carry its burden of showing that, even absent that intent, it would have made the same decision. Thus, it's likely that the court will not consider this a discrimination against gays.

ii. Applying the Appropriate Test: Assuming it's not discriminating against gays, the ethical canon would be reviewed under the most deferential rational basis test, applied to social and economic legislation (Fritz v. RR Retirement Board (1980)). The analysis here would probably be the same as under substantive due process rational basis test, explained above, with the result that A and A would lose.

However, if the court found that this was discrimination against gays, then it might apply the heightened rationality test from Romer. Even here, though, A and A might lose. The Court in Romer stressed the broad disability the statute in that case imposed on gays; by contrast, here, there is just a burdening of gays with regard to one area, access to one form of reproduction. Although there's always a chance that the Court would be more strict here, especially given that the subject matter is at least close to a fundamental right, the most likely result is that A and A would still lose.

Conclusion: A and A probably lose their equal protection claim.

CONSTITUTIONAL LAW ESSAY EXAM #5

QUESTION #1

I. Ackerman v. LSU

1. Intentional Discrimination   The claim is one of racial discrimination. However, before the appropriate level of scrutiny can be decided, it must be determined whether LSU was intentionally discriminating on the basis of race. Under the Fourteenth Amendment, a state discriminates on the basis of race only when it intentionally classifies on that basis (Washington v. Davis (1976)).

To establish intent, the following steps are taken:

1. The plaintiff must start by proving that race was one of the reasons he was denied a spot in the entering class.
2. If he shows this, then LSU must prove that it would have taken the same action anyway, even in the absence of that intent.
3. If LSU makes that showing, then the decision gets only rational basis review; if not, then the decisions would be race discrimination that would get strict scrutiny.

Discrimination can be shown by a variety of sources, including legislative history, a history of previous discrimination, the disparate impact of the discrimination and its foreseeability, and substantive or procedural deviations from normal government decision-making (Metro. Housing Corp. v. Village of Arlington Hts. (1977)).

Here, several of these factors are present. There is a history of discrimination, although that history is of anti-black, not anti-white, discrimination. The minutes of the meeting indicate the foreseeability of the racially disparate impact of the action, as well as the raw fact that it will have racially disparate impact. There is also a procedural deviation, although it seems to have the innocent explanation of needing to act quickly to prepare the admissions materials. Most likely a court would find that Ackerman met his burden.

The next step would require LSU to prove that, absent the discriminatory motive, it still would have made the same decision. This might be hard for LSU to prove, given that the minutes indicate an awareness of changing Supreme Court doctrine about affirmative action, and a desire to continue providing affirmative action under another guise, even though here too the evidence is ambiguous.

Most likely a court would find that LSU had not carried its burden, and that LSU had intentionally classified on the basis of race.

2. Level of Scrutiny   Race classifications get strict scrutiny (Grutter v. Bollinger (2003); Gratz v. Bollinger (2003)). But strict scrutiny does not mean an automatic strike-down (Grutter). In Grutter the Court upheld the state law school's affirmative action plan because it treated race as one factor of many that increased the diversity of the student body, because the admissions plan involved evaluating each student as an individual rather than simply as a member of a racial group, and because the Court decided that racial diversity in law school education was a compelling government interest. By contrast, in Gratz the Court struck down the undergraduate admissions plan because it automatically granted points based on membership in a racial group.

The LSU plan looks more like the law school plan upheld in Grutter than the undergraduate plan struck down in Gratz. Even though the LSU plan is dealing with undergraduates, nevertheless, like the plan in Grutter, it evaluates students individually, and treats race as only one diversity factor among many. As long as the Court is willing to consider diversity in undergraduate admissions as compelling an interest as diversity in law school admissions, this plan has a good chance of surviving strict scrutiny.

Conclusion: The LSU plan will probably be upheld.

II. Bride v. State

1. Free Speech/Incitement   The question here is whether Bride's speech is protected by the First Amendment. In Brandenburg v. Ohio (1969) the Court held that speech could be prohibited as inciting illegal activity only when the speaker intended to incite immediate unlawful conduct and the speech was likely to be successful in doing so. In subsequent years the Court has applied this test in a speech-protective manner (Hess v. Indiana (1974); NAACP v. Claiborne Hardware (1982)).

Here, Bride will probably win his claim that the First Amendment protects his speech. It's clear that he is not arguing that unlawful activity should take place at that moment; rather, his speech is clearly of the abstract, though impassioned, sort. He made no suggestion that students do anything at that moment; his reference to patience running out must be seen as abstract oratory. Moreover, it's not even clear whether, objectively, such unlawful conduct was likely to result. There were counter-protesters in the area; thus, there may be some argument that violence was likely. But a student shoving a book into someone's face is hardly a natural result of a speech in which the speaker talks of "shoving the Constitution into white people's faces." Even if this prong goes against Bride, he will still win because both prongs are necessary for a valid conviction.

Conclusion: Bride will probably be set free.

III. BSU v. LSU

1. Associational Rights   This question implicates BSU's associational rights. Individuals have rights to associate, both intimately and for expressive reasons, and restrictions on that right will be reviewed strictly (Roberts v. Jaycees (1984)).

In this case, BSU probably doesn't have intimate associational rights. Intimate associations are marked by their small size and selectivity (Roberts). Here, BSU is open to all African-American students at LSU, presumably not a small number of people; moreover, there are no membership criteria except race. In addition, the BSU by-laws note that it will open its social gatherings to all.

However, BSU probably does have a claim to expressive association. The Court has recognized that individuals have rights to associate in order to promote certain viewpoints, e.g., political parties, rifle clubs, and other similar-type groups.

Unlike in Roberts, in which it was unclear whether the Jaycees took any positions that were marked by a distinctive male viewpoint, a court might be sympathetic to the idea that African-Americans might want to associate among themselves to develop and present a distinctive African-American viewpoint on issues. Under Dale v. Boy Scouts (2000), claims by a group that it espouses particular viewpoints will be granted deference.

On the other hand, the court would surely credit LSU's desire to minimize racial antagonism by ensuring that members of different races talk together. However, under Roberts the Court would ask whether this plainly legitimate goal could be met by a means less intrusive on associational rights. Here, that goal could have been met by the school creating forums for interracial dialogue.

Conclusion: BSU probably wins its claim of associational rights.

QUESTION #2

I. Boulevard Investments v. City of Los Angeles

1. Takings   BI could conceivably have claims based on the Takings Clause and the Contracts Clause.

Even a compensated taking is unconstitutional if the property is not taken for a public interest. However, this is a very lenient standard, as the Supreme Court recognizes that legislatures are best suited to determining what the public interest requires. (Hawaii Housing Authority v. Midkiff (1984)). Urban revitalization would surely constitute a valid public purpose.

The ordinance does not formally take BI's property, in the sense of physically appropriating or taking title. Instead, if it takes at all, it is by regulating the property. A regulation that goes too far will be considered a taking (Penn. Coal v. Mahon (1922)). Courts use a multi-factor fact-intensive test to determine whether a regulatory taking has occurred. Factors that are relevant include the amount of value of the property that is lost, the loss of the owner's investment-backed expectations, and the extent to which the action singles out one property owner rather than spreading the burden across a class of property owners (Penn Central Trans. Corp. v. New York City (1978)).

Here, the regulation is clearly broad-based, not singling out BI. Moreover, BI can still use its properties as storefront rentals, as long as it rents them to the right type of business. The amount of loss BI suffers is not clear from the facts. However, there is at least an argument that a revitalized Hollywood Boulevard will lead to higher rents. Even without that speculation, though, the other factors suggest that there is no taking here.

Conclusion: BI would lose a takings claim.

2. Contracts Clause   Assuming there is an impairment, the Contracts Clause does not prohibit any impairment of contracts, because much government action impairs contractual rights in one way or another. Thus, the general rule has developed that only substantial impairments will be scrutinized (Allied Structural Steel v. Spannus (1976)). If the impairment is deemed substantial, then it will be scrutinized more carefully the greater the impairment.

Here there is at least a question whether the ordinance directly abrogates contracts, because potentially the lessees could operate other types of businesses under their current leases. However, the facts suggest that the leases call for certain types of businesses to be conducted on the premises, thus suggesting that there may be impairment.

The impairment may or may not be substantial. We are not told how valuable the leases are. However, if the leases are long-term, then the impairment could be akin to that in Allied, where the government action changed an employer's pension funding obligation, a commitment the long-term nature of which the Court noted.

In this case, the city probably will be held to have a substantial interest in impairing these contracts, because it wants to redevelop part of the city. Although the balancing between the substantiality of the impairment and the importance of the government interest is inherently case-specific, there is a good argument here that the city's interest would outweigh the interests of BI.

Conclusion: BI would probably lose the impairment claim.

II. Shady v. City of Los Angeles

1. Free Speech/Secondary Effects Regulation The restriction on Sam's business would probably be considered a regulation relating to the secondary effects of his businesses. Under City of Renton v. Playtime Theaters (1986), such restrictions must be unrelated to the content of the speech and must leave room for the speech to occur somewhere, although this latter requirement is interpreted leniently. Here, the city's findings about these businesses, reflected in the ordinance itself, would be enough to justify a court that the ordinance was unrelated to the content of the speech. Moreover, the location requirement is not as burdensome as the one accepted in Renton, in which the restriction effectively left operators of adult theaters with less than 5% of the city area in which to locate.

Conclusion: Sam will lose his claim that the ordinance violates his free speech rights.

III. Center for Immigrant Rights v. City of Los Angeles

1. Free Speech/Speech in Public Forums The CIR would have a good argument that the ordinance violates the First Amendment by imposing a content-based restriction on speech in the traditional public forum of a street. The ordinance bans political marches but not other marches or parades, and thus is content-neutral. Even though there may not be an invidious reason behind this distinction — that is, even though the reason for this distinction does not lie in a desire to squash speech because of dislike of the content — such restrictions are still disfavored and get strict scrutiny by courts.

It is unlikely that the ordinance could survive strict scrutiny. Keeping a family-friendly atmosphere is not a compelling government interest that would justify a content-based restriction on speech, especially political speech, which is at the core of the First Amendment. Even if it were, there would be less speech-restrictive ways of taking care of the problem, such as scheduling such marches for evenings, when families and children would be less likely to be on the street.

Conclusion: The ordinance's restriction on political marches would be struck down.

QUESTION #3

I. Bennett v. Decatur School District

1. Procedural Due Process   The question is whether Bennett was denied his procedural rights under the Due Process Clause. Under that clause, individuals are entitled to a certain degree of process before government can deprive them of life, liberty, or property. To resolve that question, one needs to determine that the individual

   a. had a liberty or property interest;
   b. that was deprived; and
   c. that he didn't get adequate process.

Mathews v. Eldridge (1976).

Liberty or property interest?: Under Roth v. Bd of Regents (1972) a person has a liberty or property interest if government gives him a reasonable expectation that he will continue to enjoy a benefit as long as he meets the stated criteria. Here, it's clear that Bennett has a liberty interest in his education, because the school manual gives him the reasonable expectation that he can attend as long as he follows the rules laid down in the manual (Goss v. Lopez (1976)).

Deprivation?: Here, it's clear that Bennett was deprived of his interest when he was expelled.

Indeed, under Goss even a suspension required the Supreme Court to determine whether the student received adequate process. An expulsion would also count as a deprivation.

Adequate Process?: In Mathews the Court laid down a three-part balancing test to judge the adequacy of the procedure afforded an individual. The test balances

   a. the importance of the interest to the class of recipients;
   b. the risk of error in the current procedures, and the possibility of improved accuracy if more procedure is provided; and
   c. the government's interest.

Mathews v. Eldridge (1976).

Here, an education at one's regular high school is most likely quite important, in terms of education and social matters. Even a half-semester expulsion will probably set the student back educationally and taint him in the eyes of his teachers and classmates.

With regard to the second prong, the manual provides for no process at all until half a semester has passed. Undoubtedly an oral hearing before the expulsion would lead to more accurate decision-making. The question at issue—did the student engage in violent behavior—will most likely be illuminated by oral testimony, because such issues often turn on recollections and credibility. Finally, the government's interest in avoiding the process is not so great. Most students will probably seek readmission; thus, the government would have to convene a hearing at some point anyway and there's no money saved by delaying the hearing. Moreover, it might even be argued that the government has an indirect interest in accurate decisions, because inaccurate ones unfairly punish students and harm their education, with all the attendant bad social consequences. In Cleveland v. Loudermill (1979) the Court recognized that inappropriate termination of a government employee harmed the government, by taking a good worker off the payroll and contributing to unemployment.

Conclusion: Bennett clearly has been deprived of a constitutionally protected interest and has been afforded inadequate process. He will win his due process claim.

II. Jackson v. City of Decatur

Jackson has two arguments: first, that the no-march ordinance is unconstitutional, and second, that his arrest for incitement violates his freedom of speech.

1. Free Speech/Speech in Public Forums   The no-march ordinance is constitutionally problematic because it is a content-based speech restriction in a traditional public forum of the street. The minutes of the meeting make it clear that the city council intended the ordinance to be content-based, even if they took pains to make sure it was not viewpoint-based. Still, content-based restrictions in the traditional public forum of the street are subject to the strictest scrutiny.

Here, it is unlikely that the city could prevail in showing that its ban on marches was the least speech-restrictive way to take care of a compelling government interest. There is surely a compelling interest in public safety, but the minutes of the meeting suggest that civic embarrassment, rather than public safety, was motivating the city council. But even if a court credits an interest in public safety, there are less speech-restrictive ways of taking care of the problem. More police could be posted, or opportunities could be given for both sides to march, perhaps at different times. Shutting down speech to preserve order will probably not be allowed, especially when the shutdown is content-based.

Conclusion: The ordinance would probably be struck down.

2. Free Speech/Incitement   The issue here is whether Jackson can be prosecuted for his speech. The rule is provided by Brandenburg v. Ohio (1969), which states that, for speech to be subject to prosecution for inciting unlawful conduct, the speaker must have intended to incite such conduct as an immediate consequence of the speech (i.e., not at some indefinite later point) and that the speech have been objectively likely to succeed in doing so. The Court has generally been very speech protective in applying this test (e.g., Hess v. Indiana (1974); NAACP v. Claiborne Hardware (1982)).

Here, it's unlikely that either prong of this test would be met. Jackson's speech about including blacks in the educational process can in no way be seen as a call to immediate unlawful action. This is a classic example of abstract advocacy that is protected by the First Amendment under Brandenburg. Moreover, it's objectively unlikely that a crowd hearing such an abstract speech would take his speech literally and react violently. Although the facts are unclear, there's no reason to think that a rally in front of a school has the likelihood of turning violent, especially when the topic of the speech is the importance of all children getting an education. But even if the second prong is satisfied, the first prong will most likely be not, and thus Jackson's speech would be held protected.

Conclusion: Jackson would be innocent of incitement.

III. Elsie v. Decatur

1. Contracts Clause   This question raises an issue under the Contracts Clause. Note that it does not raise a question of the substantive due process right to contract; the Due Process Clause protects against interference with future contractual relationships, while this issue is one of interference with existing contracts.

There is a question whether this statute even impairs a contractual obligation at all, because it is not aimed at such obligations, but instead imposes a general law that has some impact on Elsie's contractual terms. In other words, the government's action does not actually force a change in contractual relations; Elsie could still carry out the terms of the contract, she just couldn't sell the product in her store as easily.

Assuming there is an impairment, the Contracts Clause does not prohibit any impairment of contracts, because much government action impairs contractual rights in one way or another. Thus, the general rule has developed that only substantial impairments will be scrutinized (Allied Structural Steel v. Spannus (1976)). If the impairment is deemed substantial, then it will be scrutinized more carefully the greater the impairment.

In determining whether and how substantial the impairment is, the Court will generally look at the raw degree of impairment, as well as the extent to which the government action upsets the parties' reasonable expectations. Once the substantiality of the impairment is determined, the Court will then balance that impairment against the state's interest.

Here, the impairment seems substantial, at least in relation to Elsie's own small-scale business. Her loss equals 1% of her gross receipts and 10% of her net income. On the other hand, the Court in Allied found the impairment there to be substantial in part because it changed the parties' long-term commitments, namely, the employer's pension funding obligations. Here, the impairment is only of a short-term obligation; once business picks up again Elsie can resume her normal form of business. Thus, there is a chance the Court will consider the impairment insubstantial.

Even if it considers the impairment substantial, the Court may well allow it, given the importance of maintaining order in the community. In Allied the Court questioned the need for the government's impairment of the parties' obligations. Here, the government has a strong argument that such impairments, even assuming they exist, are necessary.

Conclusion: Elsie probably loses her claim.

CONSTITUTIONAL LAW ESSAY EXAM #6

QUESTION #1

I. Can the Statute Be Applied to Dan?

This raises a question of congressional power to regulate interstate commerce. There's no regulation of a more specialized activity (e.g., bankruptcy or immigration) that would call to mind the more specialized congressional powers in Article I, nor is the taxing and spending power implicated. Finally, it's a stretch to say that Congress is attempting to enforce any Fourteenth Amendment rights; at any rate, the statute doesn't regulate state action, which under current doctrine is a prerequisite for congressional use of its enforcement power.

Under current doctrine, Congress can use its commerce power to regulate the following types of activities:

1. Channels of interstate commerce;
2. Instrumentalities of interstate commerce; and
3. Activities that substantially affect interstate commerce.

Here, only the third possibility might support congressional regulation. The first two require interstate activity, but under the facts nothing and nobody is moving interstate.

The test for activities that substantially affect interstate commerce turns on whether the activity being regulated is economic. If it is, then the court asks whether Congress could have had a rational basis for believing that, in the aggregate, the regulated activity has a substantial effect on interstate commerce. This is a very deferential test, as suggested by cases such as Wickard v. Fillburn (1942) and Katzenbach v. McClung (1964) which uphold congressional regulation of small-scale local activities based on this standard.

If the activity is not economic, then a court would ask whether the statute had a jurisdictional hook (i.e., some statutory element that required a closer connection to interstate commerce before an activity would fall within the statute's purview), or whether the statute was an essential part of a broader scheme of economic activity. Congressional findings about the connection between the activity and interstate commerce might also be useful, but in United States v. Morrison (2000), the Court questioned how probative such findings would be.

The definition of "economic activity" was provided in Gonzalez v. Raich (2005). It's a very broad definition, covering, among other things, the consumption or production of a good or service. Certainly a commercial pet kennel providing boarding services would come under this definition. However, Dan is arguing that the statute cannot be applied to him in particular, because he is providing those services for free. Nevertheless, Raich concluded that the possession and cultivation of marijuana for personal consumption constituted economic activity. For this reason, a court would probably use the rational basis test described above.

Applying that test to this case makes clear that application of the statute to Dan is constitutional. Congress could easily have had a rational basis for believing that, in the aggregate, ensuring that pet boarders use due care in caring for the animals entrusted to them. Such care might increase the consumption of goods, such as pet food, that would travel in interstate commerce. Even more clearly, such care might lead more Americans to entrust their pets to boarders, thus freeing them up to travel more across state lines.

Conclusion: The court would probably deny Dan's motion.

II. Would the Court Require Dan to Have His Claim Heard in Front of the Board?

This question raises an issue of the extent to which Congress can take jurisdiction away from Article III courts and place it in non–Article III courts (so-called "agency courts" or "Article I courts"). The issue arises because Article III places "the judicial power" in Article III courts. In Commodities Futures Trading Corp. v. Schor (1986) the Court set forth a three-part balancing test to decide such issues. The three factors are

1. The extent to which the agency court possesses the attributes of an Article III court, and, conversely, the extent to which Article III courts retain ultimate control over the issues litigated in the agency court. Factors that are relevant here include
   a. The availability of Article III court review of the agency court's decisions, and the standard of review the Article III court applies to those decisions;
   b. The scope of the agency court's jurisdiction (i.e., is it confined to a specialized area of law or is it general); and
   c. The types of powers the agency court has (e.g., does it have the power to enforce its own decisions and conduct jury trials).
2. The nature of the right being litigated (i.e., whether it is a private right or a public right); and
3. The reasons Congress had for taking away jurisdiction from the Article III court.

Factor 1: Here, the first factor leads to mixed results. Article III courts have the power to review the agency court's fact-findings and legal conclusions, but only under the deferential "clearly erroneous" standard. According to Schor, such a deferential standard might be appropriate for review of fact-findings, but might be problematic as applied to review of the agency court's legal conclusions. Second, the agency court has jurisdiction that parallels that the Court found acceptable in Schor, extending to "all claims arising under this statute and any other legal claims related to a plaintiff's claims under [the] statute." Although this aids the statute's constitutionality, in this case the agency's court's jurisdiction is exclusive, rather than permissive; in other words, it requires, rather than simply allows, Dan to bring his claim in the agency court. This goes beyond the scheme in Schor and might cut against the statute's constitutionality. Finally, the Article III court has exclusive power to enforce the agency court's orders; this cuts in favor of the statute's constitutionality.

Factor 2: Under this factor, it cuts against the statute's constitutionality if the claim forced to be litigated in the agency court is a private right. It's not completely clear what a private right is, but in its purest form, it's a right between two private parties (rather between a private party and the federal government) based on the common law. Dan's common-law property claim is exactly that. Because Dan's claim is a private right, this cuts against the constitutionality of the statute.

Factor 3: Under this factor if Congress strips Article III power for a legitimate reason this will favor the statute's constitutionality. A "bad" reason might be a desire to punish the courts for deciding cases a certain way, while a "good" reason might be, as in Schor, to provide a quick and convenient way of resolving certain claims that require specialized knowledge on the part of the judge. Here, all we have to go on is the congressional finding that federal courts have "undervalued" the importance Americans have placed on their relationship with their pets. This might suggest that Congress is stripping Article III courts of jurisdiction over these cases to force a different set of results (here, higher damages awards). Although it's not certain, this fact might cut against the constitutionality of the statute.

Conclusion: With factor 1 mixed, factor 2 cutting against the statute, and factor 3 potentially cutting against it, this case presents a situation in which a court might well find the Schor test to have not been satisfied. Although it's not completely clear, a court may well rule in favor of Dan's second motion.

QUESTION #2

I. State Action

1. The basic rule is that the Fourteenth Amendment applies only to states. Thus, it must be determined whether Hilldale's actions are attributable to the State of Wisconsin.
2. The black-letter categories of state action:
   a. Government function: Is the running of an adoption service akin to operating a company town (Marsh v. Alabama (1946)) or running a political primary (Terry v. Adams (1953))? It's doubtful, given the tradition of purely private adoption agencies.
   b. Legislative/Administrative approval of the private action: Is the state somehow expressing approval of the anti-gay discrimination practiced by Hilldale? It's possible that a court would find such approval in the state requirement that Hilldale make decisions about parental fitness. If Wisconsin approves of Hilldale's decisions about who is fit to be a parent, then those decisions might be attributable to the state. On the other hand, all the state requires is that the facility make a determination that, *in its opinion*, the prospective parents are fit. This qualifier might be enough to distance the state from the substance of any judgments made by Hilldale.
   c. Judicial approval of the private action: This is not an issue, as there's no judicial action here.

d. Is the state "entangled" with the private conduct? The state's regulation of adoption agencies might be thought of as entangling it with Hilldale's conduct. But even aggressive applications of this principle, such as in Burton v. Wilmington Parking Authority (1961), stressed how the state was entangled not just with the private entity in general, but with the particular discriminatory conduct complained of. Here it's not clear how closely Wisconsin is involved with Hilldale's discrimination, although, as discussed under legislative approval, above, an argument could be made.

Conclusion: State action is a very fact-dependent doctrine. Here, there might be arguments about legislative approval and entanglement, but these are by no means sure things.

II. Substantive Due Process

Assuming that state action is present, the couple may have a substantive due process argument that they are being deprived of their due process right to be foster parents. There are several different theories about how to approach substantive due process claims.

1. One Approach asks whether the right at issue is one deeply valued in American history. If it is, then the court would apply strict scrutiny to the deprivation of the right, asking if the government is attempting to promote a compelling interest in a way that has the minimum possible effect on exercise of the right. If it is not, the court would simply ask if the government has a rational basis for believing that infringement on the right would further a legitimate government interest.

In applying this rule, some justices will characterize the right as narrowly as possible, to avoid the possibility of judges simply importing their own values and preferences into the analysis (e.g., Michael H. v. Gerald D. (1989)).

If a court applied this rule, it would ask whether foster parentage by a gay couple is a right deeply valued in American history. It is likely that question would be answered in the negative, and that, using rational basis review, the government would have a rational basis for believing that infringing on this right would further the legitimate government interest of, for example, ensuring that children are placed with couples who have the possibility of getting married (assuming that same-sex marriage is not allowed in that state). Note that the rational basis test is very lenient, thus allowing the court to engage in any kind of speculation about interests the state may wish to attempt to further.

Other justices might characterize the right more broadly, as, say, the right of adults to be parents, or to be foster parents. If a court took this approach, it might find the right to be fundamental and apply strict scrutiny, which might be more difficult for the government to overcome.

2. A Second Approach, one endorsed by Justice Harlan in Poe v. Ullman (1961) and Justice Souter in Washington v. Glucksberg (1997), features a more free-floating reasonableness inquiry, which asks if the government acted reasonably in deciding that the public interest required an imposition on the right. This view looks at history when determining the importance of the right at issue, although it also considers how that history is evolving. This view is less rigid than the fundamental/non-fundamental right analysis described above, but in application it is similar. In applying this test, a court might find that the evolution of state laws to allow same-sex couples significant rights, including parental rights, reflected an evolving tradition in favor of those rights that might render the state's decision unreasonable.

3. Finally, in Lawrence v. Texas (2003) Justice Kennedy applied something more than rational basis review to strike down Texas's sodomy law under substantive due process. In particular, this test does not feature courts hypothesizing connections between the deprivation of the right and a legitimate state interest. It also does not allow mere moral disapproval to justify such deprivations. In determining the importance of the interest, Justice Kennedy did a "history and tradition" analysis, but focused on the last 50 years. Under this test, just as with the Harlan/Souter test, the evolving nature of the rights enjoyed by same-sex couples in the marriage and family area might lead a court to conclude that the state law is unconstitutional, unless the state could present empirical evidence that depriving the right to Anderson and Baker serves a public purpose beyond merely expressing moral disapproval of gays and lesbians. As with the Harlan/Souter approach, however, this approach is vague and its results can be unpredictable.

QUESTION #3

I. State Action

The first question to be answered is whether there is state action. The IFC is a private entity; however, there may be several theories by which its recommendations can be attributed to the state:

1. Public Function: The IFC may constitute a state actor because it is performing a public function, similar to the privately owned company town in Marsh v. Alabama (1946) or the private political group that ran a political primary in Terry v. Adams (1953). Here, the IFC drafts recommendations that, by virtue of state law, become the rule of decision in certain court cases. In essence, then, the IFC is arguably acting like a lawmaker, a quintessential sovereign function. It thus may be a state actor under this theory.

2. Legislative Approval: The same fact — that the legislature has deemed the IFC's recommendations to be the rule of decision in certain court cases — would also support a conclusion that the recommendations have been approved by the state. Similar to Reitman v. Mulkey (1967), the state has put its approval on particular private conduct, in this case even more explicitly by giving the IFC the authority to write legally binding rules.

3. Judicial Approval: The court's adoption of the IFC's recommendations could also be seen as an instance of courts approving of the views expressed by the recommendations. Just as in Shelly v. Kraemer (1948), the court here would be using these privately drafted rules to decide a case.

4. Entanglement: Finally, one could use these same facts to craft an argument that the state is entangled with the IFC's recommendations. By delegating lawmaking power to the IFC, it could be argued that the state is in a symbiotic relationship with the IFC, benefiting from the latter's expertise. This might be enough to justify a finding of entanglement, although it may be that the public function and legislative approval theories are stronger because they're more direct.

II. Equal Protection Claims

Sonia may have two viable equal protection claims — one based on gender discrimination and the other on sexual orientation.

1. Gender   Gender is a possible theory because the recommendation's preference for fathers over mothers clearly burdens Sonia based on her gender.

a. Intent: Under Washington v. Davis (1976), equal protection claims require intentional discrimination by the government. Here, intent is satisfied because the statute facially distinguishes between mothers and fathers, thereby classifying based on gender.

b. Standard of Review: Gender classifications must satisfy intermediate scrutiny — that is, they must be substantially related to further an important government interest (Craig v. Boren (1976)). Gender classifications must not reflect outmoded stereotypes about gender roles or characteristics (Miss. U. for Women v. Hogan (1982); United States v. Virginia (1996)). The purpose offered must be the government's actual purpose, not a hypothetical one (Virginia). However, classifications designed to compensate women for past discrimination may be allowable (Virginia).

c. Application of the Standard: Here, the minutes of the meeting reflect at least some stereotypical thinking on the part of at least one board member. Moreover, the memo by the archivist suggests that stereotypes about men and women (and boys and girls) underlay the original version of the recommendation. The fact (noted in the memo and the minutes) that the reasons for the recommendation were never revisited suggests that no more acceptable justification was ever adopted for the paternal preference. Against all this, the state can probably offer little except the expertise of the IFC in determining whether real differences exist between fathers and mothers in this context. However, the lack of any finding to this effect by the IFC, except for the stereotyped reasons expressed in the original recommendation and one of the board members, probably means this justification will be rejected, just as the Court in Virginia rejected the state's argument that real gender differences justified keeping women out of VMI.

For these reasons it is likely that the recommendation will be struck down as unconstitutional gender discrimination.

2. Sexual Orientation   Sonia may also have an argument that the recommendation discriminates based on her sexual orientation, because it makes it impossible for a lesbian ever to gain a preference under the recommendation (as she would have to be in a relationship with a man for the recommendation to be neutral as between the mother and the father).

a. Intent: Unlike with the gender claim, however, the sexual orientation claim requires an investigation into intent. Although it's arguable that the sexual orientation discrimination is evident on the face of the recommendation, it takes enough teasing out from the recommendation's implications to suggest that a court may not find the recommendation to facially classify on this basis.

b. The Intent Analysis: In Village of Arlington Heights v. Metro. Housing Development Corp. (1977) the Court set forth the basic structure for intent analysis.

First, the plaintiff has the burden of proving that the alleged grounds of classification (here, sexual orientation) was one of the factors motivating the government's action. If she shows that, then the burden shifts to the government to prove that it would have made the same decision, even if it had not been motivated by the alleged grounds. If the plaintiff fails at the first phase or the defendant succeeds at the second phase then the intent requirement is not satisfied.

Second, the Court also set forth a number of factors the plaintiff can cite when making her intent argument:

1. The extent of the disparate impact caused by the government action;
2. The foreseeability of that impact;
3. The legislative history of that action;
4. The extent to which the action was marked by any substantive or procedural deviations from normal practice; and
5. The historical background of the decision (e.g., whether that actor had a history of discriminating on these grounds).

3. Applying the Intent Analysis Applying these factors, Sonia can probably make her initial showing. First, the recommendation has serious disparate impact based on sexual orientation, as discussed above. Second, the minutes make clear that the board was aware of this impact — thus, it was foreseeable. Third, the legislative history suggests that at least one board member favored the recommendation at least in part because it burdened lesbians. Fourth, there is a deviation from normal procedure: Usually the board discusses a recommendation then votes only at a subsequent meeting, whereas here the discussion and vote happened at the same meeting. There is no substantive deviation apparent from the facts, nor does there appear to be a history of intentional discrimination on this ground, as noted in the memo (although the memo does suggest that earlier board members simply could not conceive of a lesbian being a mother, which might be taken to suggest discriminatory attitudes). Given this evidence, Sonia can probably make her preliminary showing.

Can the government make its showing that it would have made the same decision even absent the discriminatory intent? Possibly. One of the board members who was in the 2-1 majority wonders out loud whether they're making "the right decision for the wrong reason." He also cites some evidence for the rule that goes beyond discriminatory attitudes. This might suggest that there were good, non-discriminatory justifications for the recommendation that would have carried the day even in the absence of the discriminatory intent. This is a close question.

If the court decides that the government carried its burden then Sonia's sexual orientation claim is defeated. Otherwise, the next question is the proper standard of review.

4. The Standard of Review   The Court has never decided the standard of review to be applied to claims of sexual orientation discrimination. Thus, it will have to consider the factors used to determine suspect class status:

1. History of discrimination: It's pretty clear that gays and lesbians have suffered a history of discrimination; most courts to have considered the issue have so concluded.
2. Immutability/Relevance of the characteristic: Courts have disagreed on the immutability point. Some have suggested that sexual orientation is not immutable, as it is a behavior rather than a pure status. Others note the biological foundations of sexual orientation, while still others conclude that sexual orientation is basic enough to one's personhood that it is for all intents and purposes immutable. Finally, courts have disagreed on the relevance of sexual orientation, much as American society disagrees.
3. Political powerlessness: Again courts have disagreed, with some courts pointing to legislative victories gays have won to conclude that they are not powerless, while others note continued discrimination gays face and thus conclude that gays continue to need judicial protection.

Conclusion: Very difficult to know how a court would come out. At most, sexual orientation would probably get intermediate scrutiny, although some state courts have given strict scrutiny based on analyses founded in their state constitutions' equal protection clauses.

5. Applying the Standard   Even if the court rejects heightened scrutiny it still might apply a more muscular, less-deferential version of rational-basis review, as it did in Romer v. Evans (1996) and Cleburne v. Cleburne Living Center (1985). This would involve less deference to the government and less willingness to hypothesize a rational basis for the government's action.

Intermediate scrutiny or even heightened rational-basis review might lead the court to strike down the statute if it believes it to be motivated by animus. One of the board's members expressed that kind of animus in the minutes, thus making it easy for the court to conclude that animus was in fact motivating the action, as in Cleburne.

CONSTITUTIONAL LAW
MULTIPLE CHOICE
115 QUESTIONS

ANSWER SHEET

Print or copy this answer sheet to all multiple choice questions.

1.	A B C D	30.	A B C D	59.	A B C D	88.	A B C D
2.	A B C D	31.	A B C D	60.	A B C D	89.	A B C D
3.	A B C D	32.	A B C D	61.	A B C D	90.	A B C D
4.	A B C D	33.	A B C D	62.	A B C D	91.	A B C D
5.	A B C D	34.	A B C D	63.	A B C D	92.	A B C D
6.	A B C D	35.	A B C D	64.	A B C D	93.	A B C D
7.	A B C D	36.	A B C D	65.	A B C D	94.	A B C D
8.	A B C D	37.	A B C D	66.	A B C D	95.	A B C D
9.	A B C D	38.	A B C D	67.	A B C D	96.	A B C D
10.	A B C D	39.	A B C D	68.	A B C D	97.	A B C D
11.	A B C D	40.	A B C D	69.	A B C D	98.	A B C D
12.	A B C D	41.	A B C D	70.	A B C D	99.	A B C D
13.	A B C D	42.	A B C D	71.	A B C D	100.	A B C D
14.	A B C D	43.	A B C D	72.	A B C D	101.	A B C D
15.	A B C D	44.	A B C D	73.	A B C D	102.	A B C D
16.	A B C D	45.	A B C D	74.	A B C D	103.	A B C D
17.	A B C D	46.	A B C D	75.	A B C D	104.	A B C D
18.	A B C D	47.	A B C D	76.	A B C D	105.	A B C D
19.	A B C D	48.	A B C D	77.	A B C D	106.	A B C D
20.	A B C D	49.	A B C D	78.	A B C D	107.	A B C D
21.	A B C D	50.	A B C D	79.	A B C D	108.	A B C D
22.	A B C D	51.	A B C D	80.	A B C D	109.	A B C D
23.	A B C D	52.	A B C D	81.	A B C D	110.	A B C D
24.	A B C D	53.	A B C D	82.	A B C D	111.	A B C D
25.	A B C D	54.	A B C D	83.	A B C D	112.	A B C D
26.	A B C D	55.	A B C D	84.	A B C D	113.	A B C D
27.	A B C D	56.	A B C D	85.	A B C D	114.	A B C D
28.	A B C D	57.	A B C D	86.	A B C D	115.	A B C D
29.	A B C D	58.	A B C D	87.	A B C D		

CONSTITUTIONAL LAW QUESTIONS

Questions 1–7 deal with the following situation:

Congress, alarmed by several incidents in which individuals attempting to purchase items over the Internet were the victims of identity theft when their credit card information was hacked into, enacts the "Internet Commerce Promotion and Protection Act" (ICPPA). The statute reads as follows:

§1. Findings: The Congress hereby finds that commerce on the Internet presents a new opportunity for economic growth, but that this growth can be realized only if potential customers can reasonably believe that Internet transactions are technologically safe and secure. The Congress also finds that Americans have the right to Internet transactions that are as secure as face-to-face transactions.

§2. Definitions:
   A. "Internet Business" means any person, corporation or other entity that customarily offers goods or services for sale on the Internet.

§3. Safety of Internet Transactions: Internet Businesses shall, to the extent feasible, ensure the maximum safety of Internet transactions.

§4. Implementation Authority: The Federal Trade Commission (FTC) is hereby authorized and directed to promulgate regulations to implement the policy reflected in §3.

§5. Legislative Oversight: Congress may overturn any regulation promulgated pursuant to §4 of this statute, upon a majority vote of both houses of Congress.

§6. Fines: Any Internet Business violating this statute or any valid regulation promulgated pursuant to §4 shall be liable for a fine of at least $5,000 per violation.

§7. Adjudication of Fines: Alleged violations of this statute or of regulations promulgated pursuant to §4 shall be adjudicated by an Administrative Law Judge (ALJ) within the FTC. Appeals from any such decision may be made to the "Internet Commerce Court," which shall be comprised of rotating panels of three federal judges. The Internet Commerce Court shall reverse any factual findings or legal conclusions found to be clearly erroneous. The decisions of this court shall be final and not subject to further review.

§8. Legal Validity: Any person may bring suit in the appropriate federal court to contest the constitutionality or other legal validity of this statute or any action taken thereunder.

Pursuant to the statute, the FTC promulgates the following regulation:

Reg. A: No Internet Business may intentionally market to minors, or knowingly accept orders from minors, without express consent from their parents or legal guardians.

1. Is §5 constitutional?

A) **YES**: Any problem with the Presentment Clause is taken care of by the fact that the agency proposing the regulations is within the executive branch; thus, the President retains his role in the lawmaking process.

B) **YES**: There is no Presentment Clause problem because Congress is passing judgment on a proposed agency regulation, which isn't "legislation" and thus doesn't require presentment.

C) **NO**: There is a Presentment Clause problem.

D) **NO**: It would be constitutional only if the statute required that two-thirds of each house veto the proposed regulation, because two-thirds would be enough to override any Presidential veto that might have otherwise been imposed.

2. The United States Chamber of Commerce sues to have the statute struck down. Which of the following arguments would probably be successful?

I. The statute violates the non-delegation doctrine.

II. The statute violates the anti-commandeering principle.

III. The statute is beyond Congress' power to regulate interstate commerce.

IV. The statute includes an unconstitutional legislative veto.

A) I and IV.

B) II and IV.

C) IV only.

D) III only.

3. Wile E. Coyote buys a jet-propelled skateboard off Acme Corporation's website, only to find that it doesn't work as advertised. He brings a common-law fraud suit in Arizona state court. Acme moves to dismiss, arguing that the ICPPA preempts state common-law tort remedies. Which of the following is the most likely result?

A) The court will deny Acme's motion to dismiss; because preemption is concerned with federalism, it acts only as a constraint on federal, not state, courts.

B) The court will probably deny Acme's motion to dismiss, on the ground that the object of the federal law is Internet security, whereas the object of the state fraud law is fair dealing in commercial transactions.

C) The court will probably grant Acme's motion to dismiss, as long as the federal law could reasonably be read as preempting the state law.

D) The court will probably deny Acme's motion to dismiss, on the ground that the ICPPA does not include a clear statement preempting state tort law.

4. The FTC brings an enforcement action against Gingrich Gadgets, Inc., a company that sells toys and games on the Internet, alleging that Gingrich violated Reg. A. Gingrich files suit in federal court, alleging that the ALJ adjudication scheme set forth in §7 violates Article III. Would Gingrich have standing to sue?

A) **YES**: All that is required for Article III standing is that Congress bestow on a party the right to sue. Because §8 does that, Gingrich has standing.

B) **YES**: As long as Gingrich can demonstrate that it was injured by the statute, and that a court order enjoining its enforcement would remedy that injury, then it could sue.

C) **NO**: Gingrich could not sue until it had attempted to sell a product in violation of the statute, and been cited for such a violation.

D) **YES**: Gingrich can sue as long as it suffered economic injury, which is the only type of injury Article III courts recognize as sufficient to confer standing.

5. Assuming Gingrich had standing, which of the following statements about its legal claims would be accurate?

I. The fact that the issue here is a private right, as opposed to a public right, strongly favors the statute's constitutionality.

II. The fact that the issue here is a private right, as opposed to a public right, is irrelevant to the constitutional inquiry.

III. The Court will apply a balancing test in determining the constitutionality of §7.

IV. The fact that no appeal is allowed from the Internet Commerce Court means that the statute is probably unconstitutional.

    A) I and III.

    B) III and IV.

    C) III only.

    D) II and III.

6. After ALJs in several unrelated cases interpret §3's "feasibility" requirement as requiring Internet businesses to conduct detailed background checks on employees who process Internet purchase orders, Congress enacts the following amendment to the bill appropriating money for the FTC's 2000 budget:

> "The Congress hereby directs and determines that employee background checks are not feasible, as that term is used in §3 of the ICCPA."

Is this amendment constitutional?

A) **NO**: It directs a fact-finding to the court, and thus violates the separation of powers.

B) **YES**: This provision is nothing more than an amendment to the underlying statute, and thus is well within Congress' power. However, Congress cannot apply this change retroactively.

C) **YES**: This provision is nothing more than an amendment to the underlying statute, and thus is well within Congress' power. Congress also has substantial power to apply this change retroactively.

D) **YES**: This provision is nothing more than an amendment to the underlying statute, and thus is well within Congress' power. Congress also has substantial power to apply this change retroactively as long as it does not try to apply this change to cases that have progressed to final judgment in the Internet Commerce Court.

7. The State of California operates a website on which it sells state maps and other paraphernalia, and thus qualifies as an "Internet Business." Does it have to comply with the statute?

A) **NO**: Imposing the law on the state would violate the anti-commandeering principle the Court has found in the Tenth Amendment.

B) **NO**: Imposing the law on the state would violate the Commerce Clause.

C) **YES**: Congress may impose generally applicable economic regulation on the states.

D) **YES**: Congress may impose on states any requirement it wishes, as long as the requirement has at least a substantial effect on interstate commerce.

8. Which of the following best describes Congress' power under §5 of the Fourteenth Amendment?

A) Although the text of §5 gives Congress the power to "interpret and enforce" the provisions of the Fourteenth Amendment, the Supreme Court has interpreted §5 so narrowly as to essentially negate the congressional power to "interpret" the amendment.

B) Although the text of §5 gives Congress the power to "enforce" the provisions of the Fourteenth Amendment, the Supreme Court has interpreted §5 so broadly as to essentially erase the difference between "interpretation" and "enforcement."

C) The text of §5 gives Congress the power only to "enforce" the provisions of the Fourteenth Amendment; and although the Supreme Court has generally read that power broadly, it has on occasion struck down statutes by holding that the given statute lacked "congruence and proportionality."

D) The text of §5 gives Congress the power only to "enforce" the provisions of the Fourteenth Amendment; and although the Supreme Court has required that statutes be "congruent and proportional" the Court has unfailingly given that power an extremely broad reading.

9. Which of the following would be the most constitutionally questionable feature of a statute providing for the naming of a special prosecutor to examine possible illegalities by a member of the executive branch?

A) A feature that allowed the President to fire the prosecutor only for "good cause" or for "physical or mental impairment that made it impossible for the prosecutor to perform his or her duties."

B) A feature authorizing a federal court to participate in the process by which the prosecutor is chosen.

C) A feature that allowed the President to fire the prosecutor because the President believed that the prosecutor did not share the policy goals of his administration.

D) A feature that authorized Congress to require the prosecutor to indict a target of the investigation whenever Congress found "unmistakable evidence" of illegalities.

Questions 10–13 refer to the following situation:

In response to the threat of domestic terrorism, Congress passes and the President signs the "Fertilizer Abuse Act." The statute reads as follows:

§1. Findings
    The Congress hereby finds that the easy availability of fertilizer, while unquestionably beneficial to the American farmer, has unfortunately provided a ready supply of the fundamental building block of homemade bombs.

§2. Fertilizer Tracing
    The manufacture of fertilizers that are readily convertible into bomb materials shall be conducted in a way so as to ensure that said fertilizers can be traced to the manufacturing plant where it was produced, to the extent feasible taking into the account the cost of ensuring such traceability.
    This section applies to all manufacturers of fertilizer, including local, state and the federal governments.

§3. Recordkeeping
    Any person who sells fertilizers that are readily convertible into bomb materials shall make and retain, for a period of five years, a record of every such sale.

§4. Spot Checks, Local Law Enforcement, and State Legislation
    The sheriff of each county in the United States shall conduct spot checks on fertilizer retailers, and during such spot checks shall examine the retailer's sales records for conformity with this statute.
    The sheriff of each county in the United States shall submit an annual report to his or her respective state legislature detailing the results of his or her spot checks, and recommending what, if any, legislative action the legislature should take to ensure that fertilizer is being sold only for legitimate purposes.

§5. Tax on Fertilizer Manufacturing
    There is hereby imposed on fertilizer manufacturers a tax of 10% on the wholesale value of any fertilizer sold.

§6. Federal Court Jurisdiction

Any person may sue in federal district court any fertilizer manufacturer or retailer who violates any provision of this statute. The court shall award damages as appropriate.

10. Is §2 constitutional?

A) **NO**, given the lack of findings tying the regulated activity to interstate commerce.

B) **YES**, given the link between fertilizer manufacturing and interstate commerce.

C) **NO**, because it regulates the activities of state governments.

D) **YES**, because this is a direct regulation of interstate commerce.

11. Is §4 constitutional?

A) **YES**, because the manufacture and sale of fertilizer substantially affects interstate commerce.

B) **NO**, the statute commandeers both the law-enforcing and law-making apparatuses of the states, in violation of the federalism principle inherent in the Tenth Amendment.

C) **NO**, the statute commandeers the law-enforcing apparatus of the states, in violation of the federalism principle inherent in the Tenth Amendment.

D) **NO**, the statute commandeers the law-making apparatus of the states, in violation of the federalism principle inherent in the Tenth Amendment.

12. Is §5 constitutional?

A) **YES**: The federal government could tax the manufacture of fertilizer only if it could also regulate it; because manufacture of fertilizer is well within Congress' Commerce Clause regulatory power, the government also has the power to tax the activity.

B) **NO**: The federal government could tax the manufacture of fertilizer only if it could also regulate it; because manufacture of fertilizer is beyond Congress' Commerce Clause regulatory power, the government does not have the power to tax the activity.

C) **YES**: The federal government's taxing power is independent of its other Article I powers; thus, even if Congress could not regulate the manufacture of fertilizer it could still tax it.

D) **NO**: The government would have the power to tax fertilizer only if it also imposed equal taxes on other materials that contributed to domestic terrorism, but because those materials were not taxed Congress does not have the power to single out fertilizer.

13. Pursuant to §6, an individual sues in federal court the State of South Dakota, whose prison system operates a fertilizer plant, alleging violation of the traceability requirement. The plaintiff also alleges violation of South Dakota tort law regarding the manufacture of ultra-hazardous products. Assume the plaintiff has standing. What result?

  I. The court would allow the plaintiff to seek damages under the federal law cause of action.

 II. The court would allow the plaintiff to seek damages under the state law cause of action.

III. The court would allow the plaintiff to seek an injunction under the state law cause of action (assume South Dakota tort law allows injunctions in this kind of case).

  A) I only.

  B) III only.

  C) II and III.

  D) None of the above.

Questions 14–16 refer to the following situation:

In 2009, the State of Iowa enacts the following statute:

§1. Findings
   The Iowa Legislature finds that commercial chicken plants generally have low safety and hygiene standards, with the result that chicken from such plants is often unfit for human consumption.

§2. Warning Labels
   Chicken from commercial chicken plants shall have the following label affixed to their packages before being offered for sale in Iowa. "WARNING: This chicken comes from a large, commercial chicken processing plant. The State of Iowa believes that such plants generally have lower health and safety standards than smaller, family-run plants."

§3. Definitions
   "Commercial chicken plant" means any chicken production plant that has the capacity to produce 1,000 pounds or more of chicken per day.

14. Which of the following facts, if true, would provide the **strongest** support for the claim that the Iowa statute **DID NOT** violate the Dormant Commerce Clause?

  A) Food poisoning from unsanitary chicken packaging operations is a legitimate public health problem.

  B) The largest Iowa chicken producer can produce only 750 pounds of chicken per day.

C) Consumer demand for chicken in Iowa is satisfied by a variety of sources, including small chicken producers (i.e., less than 1,000 pounds-per-day capacity), Iowa-based "commercial chicken plants," and out-of-state "commercial chicken plants."

D) The Federation of Iowa Consumers lobbied vigorously for the law, arguing that chicken was more dangerous than beef and required stricter regulation.

15. Which of the following facts, if true, would provide **strongest** support for the claim that the Iowa statute **DID** violate the Dormant Commerce Clause?

A) Food poisoning from unsanitary chicken packaging operations is a legitimate public health problem.

B) The largest Iowa chicken producer can produce only 750 pounds of chicken per day.

C) Demand for chicken in Iowa is satisfied by a variety of sources, including small chicken producers (i.e., less than 1,000 pounds-per-day capacity), Iowa-based "commercial chicken plants," and out-of-state "commercial chicken plants."

D) The Federation of Iowa Consumers lobbied vigorously for the law, arguing that chicken was more dangerous than beef and required stricter regulation.

16. Which of the following responses to the Iowa statute would be constitutional?

I. Arkansas, the home of most "commercial chicken plants," imposes an embargo on Iowa beef; the embargo statute states that it will automatically expire when and if Iowa repeals its chicken warning statute, or when the Iowa law is struck down by the Supreme Court.

II. Congress passes a law prohibiting states from imposing labeling requirements of the type in the Iowa statute.

III. Congress passes a law authorizing states to impose embargoes on chickens from "commercial chicken plants."

IV. No legislative action would be appropriate until the Supreme Court had decided on the constitutionality of the Iowa statute.

A) I and III.

B) I and II.

C) II and III.

D) IV only.

17. Which of the following statements about equal protection is most accurate?

A) The Supreme Court has maintained, in practice as well as in theory, a strict three-tiered approach to classifications drawn by legislatures.

B) The Supreme Court has explicitly embraced a sliding scale approach to equal protection, much more intricate and sophisticated than the earlier three-tiered approach.

C) The Supreme Court maintains a strict three-tiered approach to classifications drawn by legislatures. However, it will sometimes announce that, because of some factor raising the Court's suspicion, it is applying a more stringent version of the applicable standard.

D) The Supreme Court has purported to adhere to a strict three-tiered approach to classifications drawn by legislatures, but in practice has deviated from this strict approach.

Questions 18–19 refer to the following situation:

Susan Nichols is a secretary for Mandeville Builders, a construction firm. She applies for Mandeville's construction apprentice program, in which individuals are trained to become certified carpenters for the company. The head of the program refuses to let Susan enroll, telling her that "construction is a man's job." The program head then refers Susan to Mandeville's secretarial training program, which allows secretaries to train to become personnel supervisors, at a pay grade at least as high as that of a certified carpenter. Susan wishes to claim that Mandeville's action violated her rights under the Equal Protection Clause.

18. Which of the following statements about the state action doctrine is accurate?

  I. The contractor's actions in this question would probably constitute "state action" if the contractor did most of its work for the State of California.

  II. The contractor's actions in this question would probably constitute "state action" if state law required that construction contractors working in California apply for and receive a state license certifying that the contractor is adequately bonded (i.e., has adequate insurance).

  III. The contractor's actions in this question would probably constitute "state action" if state law required that construction contractors working in California apply for and receive a state license certifying that they operate training programs "designed to develop a vibrant construction industry in California."

  A) I and II

  B) III only

  C) II and III

  D) I and III

19. Assuming that Mandeville's denial constituted state action, which of the following would be the most likely result of Susan's equal protection claim?

A) The court would probably rule in Susan's favor, after determining that Mandeville's action was not narrowly tailored to meet a compelling state interest.

B) The court might rule against Susan, if it concluded that Mandeville could potentially have a legitimate interest that was furthered by excluding women from the carpentry program.

C) The court would probably rule in Susan's favor, after determining that Mandeville's action had the effect of perpetuating damaging stereotypes about women.

D) The court would probably rule against Susan, because the secretarial training program provided economically equal opportunities for women.

20. In 2009, noted sexologist Edith Eastheimer publishes "The Puzzled Penis," a study of male sexuality. As part of its analysis, the book includes lengthy excerpts from interviews in which heterosexual men divulge their sexual fantasies. The book creates a stir; eminent psychologists hail it as a breakthrough while others decry it as smut. Regardless, it is clear that many, if not most, purchasers of the book are primarily interested in the interviews. A jury in Jackson County, Mississippi finds the book obscene, and the judge bans its distribution or possession in the county. Which of the following statements is most accurate?

A) As long as the jury found the book to be obscene under the local community's own standards, the judge's order would be constitutional.

B) As long as the jury found that the book appealed primarily to prurient interests, the judge's order banning distribution would be constitutional, but private possession of the book would still be constitutionally protected.

C) Neither possession nor distribution could be constitutionally prohibited, because obscene speech is still speech and thus protected by the First Amendment.

D) Neither possession nor distribution could be constitutionally prohibited, because the book is acknowledged to have serious scientific merit.

21. Which of the following constitutional provisions apply against state governments?

   I. The guarantee against the impairment of contracts.

   II. The right to a jury in most civil trials.

   III. The right to be free of double jeopardy.

   IV. The right not to be tried for a criminal offense in the absence of an indictment.

   A) I, III, and IV.

   B) III only.

C) I and III.

D) All of the above.

Questions 22–24 refer to the following situation:

The California Forestry Service requires that applicants for the position of Forest Fire Fighter (FFF) stand at least 5 feet, 8 inches tall. Catherine Bisque stands 5 feet, 5 inches tall, and thus was rejected for the FFF training program. Catherine sues the Forestry Service, alleging that the height requirement violates the Equal Protection Clause.

22. Which of the following statements best describes the law governing Catherine's claim?

A) She must show that the drafters of the rule "clearly foresaw" the gender disparate effects the rule would have. If she makes this showing, the burden shifts to the Forestry Service to prove that it would have imposed the same requirement even had it not foreseen its gender effects.

B) She must show that the rule was motivated solely by a desire to classify on the basis of gender. If she makes this showing, she wins the case.

C) She must show that the Forestry Service's rule was motivated at least in part by an intent to discriminate. But even if she makes this showing, the Service can still avoid heightened scrutiny by showing that the same rule would have been enacted even absent the discriminatory intent.

D) She must show that the Forestry Service's rule had a disparate gender impact (i.e., that the rule disqualified a statistically significant greater number of women than men). But even if she makes this showing, the Service can still win the lawsuit by showing that gender played no motivating role in the decision to adopt the rule.

23. Which of the following statements is accurate?

I. Because discriminatory intent is a constitutional requirement, Congress may not allow plaintiffs to recover based solely on the disparate impact a decision may have on a protected group, even pursuant to its power under §5 of the Fourteenth Amendment.

II. The court may infer discriminatory intent from "objective" indicators that don't themselves directly reveal the state of mind of the government decision-makers.

III. Congress may abrogate the discriminatory intent requirement pursuant to its §5 power, but given federalism concerns such abrogation would apply only to discriminatory action by the federal government, not the states.

    IV. The Court may infer discriminatory intent from "objective" indicators that don't themselves directly reveal the state of mind of the government decision-makers, but may not consider historical discrimination as relevant to intent.

    A) I and IV.

    B) I, II, and IV.

    C) II only.

    D) II and III.

24. Assume that throughout Catherine's lawsuit against the Forestry Service she has not held press conferences or appeared in the media, although the lawsuit itself has focused public attention on the so-called "macho culture" within the Forestry Service. After the suit is settled out of court, the "American Freedom Fighters," a paramilitary group, publishes an article about the lawsuit in its newsmagazine Arise, asserting that she is a radical subversive with a criminal record, and whose only intention in suing the Forestry Service was to bring state governments into disrepute and thereby hasten the takeover of the United States by the United Nations. Catherine sues Arise for libel. Which of the following statements about that lawsuit is most accurate?

    A) The Constitution requires that Catherine prove actual malice on the part of Arise before she can collect punitive damages.

    B) Because Catherine is a private figure, the Constitution allows California to set whatever standard it wishes for the recovery of punitive damages.

    C) The Constitution prohibits California from allowing Catherine to collect punitive damages against Arise.

    D) The Constitution requires that Catherine prove actual malice on the part of Arise before she can collect actual damages.

Questions 25–27 refer to the following situation:

    John Jackson is an Army veteran. Since his discharge in 2007 he has received monthly checks based on his disabled veterans' status, to compensate him for the leg injuries he suffered as an infantryman during the Gulf War. Last month he received a letter from the government, informing him that his next check would be his last. The government informed him that this decision was based on the government's conclusion that he no longer qualified as disabled, given the normal duration of the type of leg injury he received. The letter informed John that he could appeal the benefit cutoff decision by submitting written information about his medical condition to the Veterans Administration (VA). The VA would then consider that information and render a decision within 9 months. If it determined that he continued to be eligible for benefits, it would pay the back benefits, with interest. John wishes to continue receiving benefits during the appeal process and to give oral testimony as to the continued existence of his disability.

25. Which of the following facts, if true, gives strongest support to the argument that John has a due process property interest in continued receipt of his benefits?

A) As a class, disabled veterans are not wealthy, and thus need their benefits to avoid significant reductions in their standards of living.

B) John's physical presence at a hearing would make it obvious that he continues to suffer from significant leg injuries.

C) It is clear that John's leg injury was more severe than the normal type associated with combat, and that he remains "disabled" for purposes of the statutory definition of "disabled."

D) The Veteran's Benefits Act specifies that disabled veterans are entitled to benefits as long as they are disabled due to military service.

26. Assuming John has a property interest in continued receipt of the veterans benefits, which of the following facts, if true, most strongly supports the argument that the VA's eligibility determination procedures **FAIL TO SATISFY** the requirements of the Due Process Clause?

A) John is not wealthy, and thus needs the benefits to avoid a significant reduction in his standard of living.

B) The physical presence of claimants at hearings often make it obvious whether the claimant continues to suffer from significant leg injuries.

C) It is clear that John's leg injury was more severe than the normal type associated with combat, and that he remains "disabled" for purposes of the statutory definition of "disabled."

D) The Veteran's Benefits Act specifies that disabled veterans are entitled to benefits as long as they are disabled due to military service.

27. Which of the following statements about John's situation is most accurate?

A) If the VA's regulations provided the termination and appeal procedures set forth in this hypothetical, John would probably be found not to have a property interest in the benefits.

B) The question whether John had a property interest in his benefits would not turn on whether the VA's regulations had set forth the investigation and termination procedures noted in this hypothetical.

C) If the statute that granted John the right to the benefits also provided for the termination and appeal procedures set forth in the hypothetical, John would not have a claim that he was constitutionally entitled to any additional procedures, because the statute would have determined the procedural expectations he could reasonably have.

D) Because the property interest was based on federal law, the Due Process Clause itself would be a possible source of the property interest that John claims he was deprived of.

28. Which of the following statements most accurately characterizes the constitutional analysis required by a statute requiring cable operators to carry PBS (the Public Broadcasting Service) as one of the operator's "basic cable" channels?

   A) Because of the invasiveness of television, as suggested by the Court's analysis of radio in Pacifica, the statute would probably be subject to strict scrutiny.

   B) Because of the heavy government regulation cable operators work under, and the scarcity of channel space even in modern cable systems, the statute would be subject to nothing more than rational-basis review.

   C) Because the statute would represent a content-based restriction on the cable operator's free expression rights, the statute would probably be subject to strict scrutiny.

   D) Because the statute aims at ensuring that there be more, rather than less, speech on core political issues, the statute would not implicate First Amendment concerns.

29. In 2009, the California Legislature enacts a statute that requires that all primary building contractors dealing with the state set aside 15% of their subcontracting on state projects to subcontractors owned by racial minorities. The statute is accompanied by the following legislative findings:

   1. The population of California is 53% racial minority but only 5% of subcontracts for state building projects went to subcontracting firms owned by minorities.

   2. Minority-owned subcontracting firms constitute only 4% of the membership of the six regional contracting associations that exist in California.

   What would be the likely result of an equal protection-based challenge to such a scheme?

   A) The court would probably **UPHOLD IT** on the authority of Bakke v. Regents of the University of California.

   B) The court would probably **STRIKE IT DOWN** unless the legislature could come up with fact-findings that were more precisely relevant than the ones noted above.

   C) The court would probably **STRIKE IT DOWN** because such racial line-drawing is always unconstitutional except in the university admissions context.

D) The court would probably **STRIKE IT DOWN** unless the state scheme was enacted to comply with a federal spending grant requiring such set-asides.

30. Which of the following actions by a federal district court, taken in response to a finding that a school district had segregated its students by race, would be the most likely to be upheld against a claim that the court had overstepped its authority?

A) Exercising control over traditionally local decisions regarding the location of new school construction and the assignment of faculty.

B) Imposing remedies that were designed to affect enrollment in a suburban school district that had not itself segregated, by making the inner-city district's academic programs more desirable and thus more attractive to students who would otherwise enroll in a suburban district school.

C) Continuing to exercise control over all aspects of a school district's operations after some aspects of those operations had been purged of the stigma of the previous segregative conduct.

D) Ordering the local authorities to impose a tax to fund improvements necessary to make all school facilities equal in quality.

31. Cindy Coldwater wishes to challenge an Oregon statute mandating a 24-hour waiting period before she can obtain an abortion. How would you describe the state of the law to her?

A) In Planned Parenthood v. Casey, the Supreme Court concluded that the Roe v. Wade opinion attached insufficient importance to the state's interest in the protection of fetal life.

B) In Planned Parenthood v. Casey, the Supreme Court allowed states to ban abortions at any time during the pregnancy, as long as there was an exception for the life or health of the mother.

C) In Planned Parenthood v. Casey, the Supreme Court made abortion a matter of purely personal choice.

D) In Planned Parenthood v. Casey the Supreme Court reaffirmed Roe v. Wade except for Roe's "undue burden" test.

32. Which of the following statements best describes the type of speech restrictions that can be imposed on public and non-public forums and private property?

I. Content-based restrictions can be imposed on speech in public forums, as long as the restriction is reasonable.

II. The only places in which viewpoint-based restrictions can be imposed are non-public forums.

III. Non-public forums are subject to the same rules about speech restrictions as apply to privately owned property.

IV. Content-based restrictions may be permissible in non–public forums.

    A) III and IV.

    B) IV only.

    C) I and IV.

    D) I and II.

33. Which of the following statements best describes the constitutional status of commercial speech?

    A) It has no constitutional protection, because it simply proposes a commercial transaction that states can regulate as they wish.

    B) It has the same constitutional protection enjoyed by core political speech.

    C) It has partial constitutional protection, with the proviso that if government has the power to prohibit the underlying transaction that is the subject of the speech, it can choose instead to take the lesser step of prohibiting speech relating to that transaction.

    D) It has partial constitutional protection, although government can impose even a content-based distinction if it has an important motivation closely linked to the speech regulation that cannot be served as well by a less speech-restrictive means.

34. Which of the following statements best describes the results of the substantive due process cases dealing with family relationships?

    A) Under current doctrine, the Supreme Court recognizes family relationships as part of the privacy guarantee found in the penumbras of several Bill of Rights provisions.

    B) Under current doctrine, the Supreme Court recognizes family relationships as a liberty interest protected by due process, but usually reads the concept of "family" narrowly, as protecting only traditional family structures (including extended blood relations).

    C) The Supreme Court recognized family relationships as a liberty interest protected by due process during the pre–1937 period, but has since rejected this position as part of its modern doctrine of deferring to legislative judgments.

    D) The Supreme Court has never recognized family relationships as constitutionally protected.

35. The State of Georgia, attempting to comply with the Voting Rights Act, attempts to draw its federal congressional districts so as to maximize the number of seats considered "safe" seats for black candidates. Which of the following statements best reflects the law concerning such districting decisions?

A) Race-conscious districting is subject to strict scrutiny if the race classification is either explicit on the face of the statute or satisfies the Washington v. Davis and Village of Arlington Heights standards for intent.

B) The Court has relaxed its normally rigid stand against race-conscious government action when it considers a districting case, but still requires that the race-conscious districting substantially advance an important government interest.

C) The Court has relaxed its normally rigid stand against race-conscious government action when it considers a districting case, but will still subject to strict scrutiny any districting decision where race was the predominant motivating factor.

D) As long as all citizens' votes count equally in the electoral process, the Supreme Court will uphold a districting decision.

36. Which of the following statements about the Establishment Clause is true?

    I. The Court's adoption and consistent application of the Lemon test has brought predictability and certainty to an area that previously had been uncertain.

    II. The Court has consistently adopted a "non-preferentialist" vision of the Establishment Clause, such that government decisions to favor religion over non-religion have rarely received serious scrutiny by the modern Court.

    III. The Court's scrutiny of religious displays on public property has often been highly contextualized, with no ironclad rule emerging.

    IV. The Establishment Clause, like the Equal Protection Clause, is primarily focused on whether government **intended** to infringe on the "non-establishment" value; if there's no bad intent, the Court applies only the most deferential scrutiny to statutes challenged as violating the Establishment Clause.

    A) III only.

    B) II and III.

    C) I only.

    D) III and IV.

37. In 2009, California amends its public accommodations law to include sexual orientation as a protected category. The term "public accommodations" is defined to include "hotel, motel, inn, campsite, or other temporary lodging." John and Martha Bates are fundamentalist Christians who own and operate a motel in Bakersfield. When a gay couple attempt to rent a room and are turned away, they sue, alleging a violation of the statute. The Bates assert that the First

Amendment right of free association gives them the right to exclude the couple. Which of the following is the most accurate statement about the court's likely reaction to this defense?

A) The court would examine whether the Bates' motel is primarily a commercial or an expressive venture. If it is the former then the court would automatically reject the Bates' First Amendment argument.

B) The court would examine, among other things, whether the state could have achieved its goals by means less restrictive of associational freedoms.

C) The statute is content-based in that it prohibits discrimination only in "public accommodations" and not other activities; for this reason the statute will be subjected to strict scrutiny.

D) The right to associate extends only to intimate associations such as family relationships; thus, unless the Bates can show that their motel is an "intimate association," the court will reject their First Amendment argument.

Questions 38–39 relate to the following situation

Sid Sidley, the owner of Sid's Disco in Santa Barbara, petitions the City of Santa Barbara for a permit to increase the size of his club. The City is concerned that an increase in the size of the club will lead to more traffic congestion, noise, fighting and other anti-social conduct. The City grants the permit, but only on the following conditions: (1) that the music played in the club be played at less than 60 decibels; and (2) that he dedicate part of his property to the public as an extension of the public bike path that runs along the back of his property.

38. Sid sues the City, claiming that condition (2) constitutes an unconstitutional taking. What is the court's likely response?

A) The court will give only rational-basis review to the conditions imposed by the City, as they represent social and economic regulation that merits only this deferential review.

B) The court will give only rational-basis review to the conditions unless Sid could show that the conditions deprived him of 100% of the value of his property, in which case the court review would include an analysis of the proportionality between the conditions and the public problems raised by the increase in the club's size.

C) The court will find that a taking has occurred, because forcing Sid to open up part of his property to an outsider constitutes a physical invasion and physical invasions are per se takings.

D) The court will give heightened review to the conditions: this will include an analysis of the proportionality between the conditions and the public problems raised by the increase in the club's size.

39. Sid sues the City, arguing that condition (1) violates his right to free speech. Which of the following statements about that claim is most accurate?

    A) Because the restriction affects Sid's speech in his club, i.e., on private property, the restriction impairs speech in a non-public forum and thus has only to be viewpoint-neutral.

    B) Because music is not speech, there is no free speech claim.

    C) Because the restriction is content-neutral, the court would analyze the restriction as a time, place, or manner restriction on speech.

    D) Because the speech at issue is one that has full First Amendment protection (i.e., it's not fighting words, obscenity, etc.), the restriction would be analyzed against a strict scrutiny standard.

40. Carla Contrary, a self-described "agitator and annoyance to the status quo," walks down Fifth Avenue in New York City wearing a denim jacket emblazoned with a photo of the World Trade Towers collapsing, under which reads the caption, "They Deserved It." Carla is arrested by New York City police officers for disturbing the peace. At trial, the prosecutor argues that her actions came within the scope of "fighting words" and thus were not constitutionally protected. Which of the following statements most accurately states how the court would respond to that argument?

    A) It would reject the prosecutor's argument and find the speech protected, because the fighting-words doctrine has been overruled and no longer exists.

    B) It would reject the prosecutor's argument and find the speech protected, unless there was evidence that the speech did in fact threaten to cause a violent reaction among bystanders.

    C) It would not even get to the fighting words argument, because the wearing of a jacket is conduct, not speech, and thus has no First Amendment protection.

    D) It would probably agree with the prosecutor's argument and find the speech unprotected.

41. Assume Carla was instead arrested while walking in Grand Central Station, a train station operated by the State of New York. Could she argue that she was in a public forum, in which more liberal free speech rules applied?

    A) The court would probably disagree, as transportation hubs are the exception to the general rule that government-owned property is a public forum.

    B) The court would probably agree, as the category of "public forums" has steadily expanded in the last 30 years as the Court has given more and more protection to free speech.

C) The court would probably disagree, as the category of "traditional public forums" has remained static, with the Court unwilling to expand it to include new types of government-owned facilities.

D) The court would probably agree, as the category of "traditional public forums" has expanded to include new types of government-owned facilities such as airports that host large numbers of people and effectively function as public crossroads.

42. The City of Miami Beach enacts an ordinance banning "ritual sacrifice of animals." A group representing adherents to a quasi-Christian sect sues, claiming that the law interferes with their rights under the Free Exercise Clause, as their religion requires the ritualistic killing of a lamb at Easter. What result is likely?

A) The plaintiffs lose: The current law of the Free Exercise Clause protects belief, but not conduct.

B) The plaintiffs lose unless they can show that the Easter sacrifice is "central" to their religion.

C) The plaintiffs win because the ordinance impairs their religious conduct; any such impairment triggers strict scrutiny, which the ordinance would probably fail.

D) The plaintiffs win, as the ordinance would probably be found to target religious conduct.

Questions 43–45 relate to the following situation:

Fred Phipps is a well-known anti-gay crusader. In June 2009, he stages a march in New York City to coincide with the city's annual gay pride celebration. At the end of the march he makes a fiery speech, in which he characterizes homosexuality as an abomination and homosexuals as "less than human, nothing more than diseased animals that deserve to be herded into pens and slaughtered for their own good and for the public health." As the speech nears its climax, several of Phipps' followers in the audience lose control and, inspired by the speech, attack and burn down the gay bookstore down the street from the rally.

In response to the melee, the police arrest Phipps for inciting a riot and for violating a city "hate speech" ordinance, reprinted below. The police also arrest his followers for arson, rioting, and assault. The prosecutor announces that he will seek a lengthier sentence than normal for the followers, based on a New York sentencing law that prohibits assault "where the victim is selected because of his/her race, gender, or sexual orientation." The New York City hate speech ordinance reads as follows:

> "Anyone who, whether by speech or conduct, intentionally denigrates an individual or group based on her/his/its race, gender, religion or sexual orientation shall be guilty of a misdemeanor and fined accordingly."

43. Can Phipps be prosecuted for inciting a riot?

A) Yes, as long as the riot was ultimately traceable to Phipps' speech.

B) No, because the facts clearly suggest that he did not intend to incite immediate lawless action.

C) Yes, because Phipps will be held to the natural results of his speech even if he did not intend those results.

D) No, because political speech is always protected due to its centrality to the First Amendment, even if it convinces people to disobey the law.

44. Which of the following statements about the hate speech ordinance is/are true?

I. The ordinance, by prohibiting speech that "denigrates," probably goes beyond a prohibition on fighting words.

II. The ordinance is content-based and on that basis is constitutionally problematic.

III. The ordinance, by restricting itself to "intentional" denigration, poses no First Amendment problem.

IV. The ordinance is content-neutral, because "denigrating" speech is not itself a type of content.

A) I and IV.

B) I and III.

C) II only.

D) I and II.

45. Can Phipps' followers be sentenced to a lengthier jail term based on the New York sentencing law?

A) Yes, because the statute is aimed at conduct, not speech.

B) No, because the statute penalizes people for their thoughts.

C) Yes, because even though the statute aims at thoughts, it is content-neutral.

D) Yes, because the statute aims at expression that is the most likely to cause a violent reaction.

Questions 46–47 refer to the following situation:

After agricultural advances allow massive increases in orange-tree yields, the orange juice market collapses. To prevent orange growers from going broke, Congress enacts a price-support scheme that sets minimum allowable prices for juice sales at each level of the distribution chain. Under this scheme, retailers (e.g., grocery stores) must pay "name-brand" juice producers (e.g., Minute Maid and Tropicana) at least 75 cents per gallon. However, the statute allows retailers to pay as little as 70 cents per gallon for juice from "off-brand" producers. There is some indication in the legislative history that Congress intended this price differential to recreate conditions in the previous unregulated market, in which off-brand producers used cheaper oranges and sold their juice at a discount. The theory is that if retailers had to pay all producers the same price, the name-brand producers' market reputation would allow them to take essentially 100% of the market. Under the statute, the grocers could pay less for the off-brand product.

46. Tropicana sues the U.S. Department of Agriculture, alleging that this statute deprives Tropicana of the equal protection of the laws because of the price differential. Which of the following reflects the court's most likely response?

A) The court would uphold the statute because the Equal Protection Clause is found in the Fourteenth Amendment, which does not apply to the federal government.

B) The court would uphold the statute as long as there was a plausible policy reason for the price differential and the statute's classification between name- and off-brand producers was not completely irrational.

C) The court would uphold the statute because the statute recreated price differentials that existed in the previously unregulated market, and thus did not create inappropriate government distinctions between similarly situated market participants.

D) The court would uphold the statute as long as the government proved that the legislative intent suggested above was the predominant motivating factor behind the statute.

47. Tropicana, joined by a national supermarket chain, also alleges in its lawsuit that the statute deprives both plaintiffs of the right to bargain freely with each other for orange juice sales. What is the court's most likely response to this claim?

A) The court would uphold the statute because the Due Process Clause provides no protection whatsoever for the freedom to contract.

B) The court would uphold the statute if the government could prove that the statute was a reasonably necessary means to resolve an important public problem.

C) The court would uphold the statute because the Contracts Clause applies only against the states, not the federal government.

D) The court would uphold the statute because today freedom to contract is not viewed as a fundamental right.

48. The government of Vermont decides to build an oil refinery to ensure that Vermont businesses and residents are not denied home heating oil supplies during periods of shortages. The government-owned refinery has published the following guidelines for potential customers:

> "From the first to the tenth day of the month the refinery will take orders for home heating oil for delivery that month. If demand exceeds supply, the following priority list will be used:
> 1. First priority will be for Vermont residences.
> 2. Second priority will be for Vermont corporations.
> 3. Third priority will be for any heating oil distributor whose customer base includes at least 65% Vermont residences or businesses.
> 4. Fourth priority will be for any other heating oil distributor, or any other purchaser."

Which of the following best describes the constitutionality of Vermont's policy?

I. The discrimination in favor of Vermont's residences at the expense of Vermont's corporations violates the Privileges and Immunities Clause.

II. Priorities 1 and 2, by discriminating in favor of Vermonters at the expense of foreigners, violate the Dormant Commerce Clause.

III. Priority 3 violates the Dormant Commerce Clause.

A) III only.

B) I only.

C) None of the above.

D) II and III.

49. Which of the following statements about Article IV's Privileges and Immunities Clause is/are correct?

I. It does not protect corporations.

II. It applies only to rights deemed "fundamental," and requires that a state provide such a right to out-of-staters only if it chooses to provide such a right to its own residents.

III. It applies only to rights deemed "fundamental," and requires that a state provide such a right to out-of-staters, regardless of whether it provides such a right to its own residents.

IV. It has been understood to have the same meaning as the Fourteenth Amendment's Privileges and Immunities Clause, with the only difference being that the Article IV clause applies to the federal government whereas the Fourteenth Amendment's clause applies to the states.

A) I and II.

B) I, II, and IV.

C) I and III.

D) I and IV.

Questions 50–53 refer to the following situation:

Congress enacts and the President signs the "Cable T.V. Access Act." The statute reads as follows:

§1. Findings: The Congress finds that Americans' access to Cable T.V. is often hampered by their limited economic means, thus denying them the benefits of the education and entertainment available on cable, while Cable T.V. operators have been able to reap unjustifiably large profits.

§2. Reasonable Rates: Any person who operates a Cable T.V. transmission facility shall offer reasonable subscriber charges to Americans of limited means.

§3. Determination of Reasonableness; Regulations: The Federal Communications Commission shall promulgate regulations to enforce the provisions of §2 of this statute. Any such regulation may be overturned by a majority vote of both houses of Congress.

§4. Private Party Recovery: Any person injured by a violation of this statute or a regulation promulgated thereunder may bring a suit in any appropriate state court that otherwise would have jurisdiction to hear common law contract causes of action with similar amounts in controversy. The United States Supreme Court may hear appeals of decisions made by a state's highest court in any case involving this statute.

50. Is §4 constitutional?

A) **YES**: Because Article III would not allow the lower federal courts to have jurisdiction over these sorts of cases, it is constitutional for Congress to place adjudicatory power in the state courts.

B) **NO**: §4 violates the Tenth Amendment's anti-"commandeering" principle.

C) **YES**: There is no problem with the anti-"commandeering" principle, due to the Supremacy Clause.

D) **NO**: Under the Tenth Amendment's "dual sovereignty" principle, the federal government is exclusively responsible for legislating, enforcing, and adjudicating its own laws, just as the states are exclusively responsible for legislating, enforcing, and adjudicating their own laws.

51. Given its size and the small population, the State of Montana operates its own Cable T.V. transmission facilities. It refuses to comply with the federal law and the FCC regulations, claiming that it is immune. Sam Neil, a resident of Montana, seeks to sue the state to force it to comply. Which of the following statements about his suit is true?

A) Because this statute is authorized by Congress' power to regulate interstate commerce, Congress may provide for the adjudication of violations in whatever court and with whatever relief it wishes.

B) Because this statute is authorized by Congress' power to regulate interstate commerce, Sam may bring a suit only in federal court unless the state consents to a suit in state court.

C) Because the statute is authorized by Congress' power to regulate interstate commerce, in the absence of state consent the only thing Sam can do is to sue the appropriate state official, rather than the state itself.

D) Because the statute is authorized by Congress' power to regulate interstate commerce, Sam can sue only the state official, and only in state court.

52. Assuming Sam can sue, what would be the result of his claims on the merits?

A) Under any reasonable understanding of the term, the state's activity is not a "traditional state function"; thus, the statute applies to Montana.

B) Because current law recognizes the problems with the "traditional state functions" test, the court would respect the state's legislative choice and not apply the statute to Montana.

C) The court would respect the state's legislative choice, but would balance it against the federal interest in ensuring universal access to Cable T.V.; the court would apply the statute to Montana only if the federal interest "clearly outweighed" the state's interest in remaining immune from federal regulation.

D) Because the statute applies evenhandedly to state and non-state operators of Cable T.V. transmission facilities, the statute would apply to Montana.

53. Assume that the FCC promulgates a regulation with which Congress disagrees. Can they constitutionally overrule it pursuant to §3 of the statute?

A) **NO**: There is a bicameralism problem.

B) **YES**: Any presentment problem is taken care of by the fact that the President signed the original bill containing §3.

C) **NO**: This would be an unconstitutional legislative veto.

D) **NO**: Congress has no power to monitor how administrative agencies administer statutes; that power is granted to the President under Article II of the Constitution.

Questions 54–55 refer to the following situation.

In 2009, the California Legislature passes a law banning private parties from selling handguns.

54. Mac Militia brings a lawsuit, alleging that the statute violates his federal constitutional right to keep and bear arms. Which of the following statements most accurately reflects the law governing such a lawsuit?

A) The lawsuit would be thrown out, because governmental regulation of private conduct does not constitute state action.

B) The lawsuit would be thrown out, because the constitutional right to keep and bear arms does not act as a limit on state governments.

C) The lawsuit might succeed if the government was unable to prove the rationality of its classification between handguns and other weapons.

D) The lawsuit might succeed on a Takings Clause theory if the statute rendered existing stocks of handgun inventory economically valueless.

55. Assume that instead of a "right to keep and bear arms" claim Mac argues that the statute unconstitutionally distinguishes between handguns and switchblades, which he argues present the same risk to public safety. What result?

A) The statute would be upheld only if the government could prove that there was a rational reason to distinguish the two.

B) The statute would be struck down only if Mac could prove that there was no rational reason to distinguish the two.

C) Because owning a weapon is a fundamental right, the statute would be upheld only if the government could show that it was necessary to serve a compelling government interest.

D) The statute would be upheld only if the government could point to a common-law foundation for its regulation.

Questions 56–57 refer to the following situation:

Ana Romero, a Mexican-American living in Seattle, brings a lawsuit on behalf of her school-age son and all other Mexican-American children living with the boundaries of the Seattle Public School District, alleging that the school district has maintained a dual system of schools, one for Latino children and one for whites.

56. Assume that no state or city law ever required the Seattle district to segregate students by race or ethnicity. Which of the following options most accurately reflects the law?

A) Ana would lose the lawsuit.

B) Ana would still win the lawsuit as long as she could show that the district's schools were in fact segregated by race or ethnicity.

C) Ana could win the lawsuit only if she could show that, despite the lack of an official segregation policy, the district nevertheless intended to segregate students by race or ethnicity.

D) Ana could win the lawsuit only if she could identify legislative history indicating that the district's decisions were motivated by an intent to segregate students by race or ethnicity.

57. Assume for the purposes of this question that Ana can win her lawsuit. To what type of relief would she be entitled?

A) The district court could order any remedy "reasonably calculated to bring about the prompt end to the segregation."

B) The district would have broad remedial powers over a number of areas, including the quality of facilities and teacher and staff assignments, but could not order reassignment of students away from their local school.

C) The district would have broad remedial powers over a number of areas, including the quality of facilities, teacher and staff assignments, and assignment of students to achieve racial balance in each school, but would probably not have the power to order remedies affecting districts other than the offending one.

D) The district would have broad remedial powers over a number of areas, including the quality of facilities, teacher and staff assignments, and assignment of students to achieve racial balance in each school, and would also have the power to order remedies affecting other school districts "if such remedies were the only reasonable way of achieving racial balance."

58. Which of the following provisions of the Bill of Rights have been incorporated?

   I. The Free Speech Clause

   II. The Cruel and Unusual Punishment Clause

   III. The Excessive Fines Clause

   IV. The Takings Clause

   A) All of the above.

   B) I and II.

   C) I, II, and IV.

   D) II only.

59. The Fresno Transit Company (FTC) is a privately owned and operated bus company operating in Fresno. It operates under a city license, the city and the company plan routes together, the city constructs bus shelters on routes served

by the FTC, and the city issues ID cards to senior citizens that have no use other than for obtaining discounts on FTC buses. The FTC also requires that Asians sit in the back of all buses. Sylvia Lau, an Asian woman, sues the FTC, alleging a violation of her equal protection clause rights. Which of the following rationales would most likely support a claim that the FTC was a state actor?

A) The FTC is a state actor because it is performing a public function, and thus is "acting like the state."

B) The FTC is a state actor because any symbiotic relationship between a private party and government is enough to make the private party a state actor.

C) The FTC is a state actor because of the degree of interconnection between the FTC and the state.

D) The FTC is a state actor because the city's actions in issuing ID cards for FTC buses, some of which may be used by senior citizens of Asian descent, constitute approval of the FTC's discriminatory conduct.

60. Which of the following is the **MOST** accurate statement about government's constitutional power to classify individuals on the basis of gender?

A) Because gender is an immutable characteristic, and because women have been the object of pervasive discrimination in the past, classifications burdening women are subject to the highest level of judicial scrutiny.

B) Because gender is an immutable characteristic, and because women have been the object of pervasive discrimination in the past, classifications burdening women are subject to the highest level of judicial scrutiny; for these same reasons, however, classifications that appear to benefit women will receive only rational-basis scrutiny.

C) Statutes that classify according to gender receive no more judicial scrutiny than other social and economic regulation.

D) Statutes that classify according to gender receive more scrutiny than social and economic regulation, but government has more leeway to classify according to gender than according to race.

61. What powers do the states have to classify based on sexual orientation?

A) In Romer v. Evans the Court elevated sexual orientation discrimination to quasi-suspect class status; thus, such classifications must substantially further an important governmental interest.

B) The Supreme Court has never held that a sexual orientation classification is unconstitutional.

C) Because states may prohibit same-sex sexual relationships, sexual orientation classifications get only rational-basis review.

D) The Supreme Court has never held that sexual orientation classifications get heightened review, although it has struck down at least one such classification.

62. The Los Angeles Police Department (LAPD) has arrested your client for drug possession. You bring a motion to suppress the evidence, arguing that it was the fruit of an unreasonable police search. Which of the following arguments should you make?

A) The LAPD is barred from engaging in unreasonable searches by virtue of the Bill of Rights.

B) The LAPD is barred from engaging in unreasonable searches by virtue of the Fourteenth Amendment to the Constitution, which explicitly incorporates all the guarantees of the Bill of Rights.

C) The LAPD is barred from engaging in unreasonable searches by virtue of the Fourteenth Amendment to the Constitution, which has been interpreted by the Supreme Court to incorporate the Bill of Rights' guarantee against unreasonable searches.

D) The LAPD is barred from engaging in unreasonable searches by virtue of the Fourteenth Amendment to the Constitution, which has been interpreted by the Supreme Court to incorporate all the guarantees of the Bill of Rights.

63. Which of the following constitutional guarantees apply against the states?

I. The right not to be deprived of life, liberty, or property without due process of law.

II. The right to a jury trial in civil cases.

III. The right not to be tried for a serious criminal offense without having first been indicted by a grand jury.

IV. The right not to have the government impair contractual obligations.

A) I, II, and IV.

B) I and II.

C) I and IV.

D) I and III.

64. Which of the following has **NOT** been identified as the source of the constitutional right to privacy underlying cases such as Griswold v. Connecticut and Roe v. Wade?

A) The Ninth Amendment.

B) The Fifth and Fourteenth Amendments' protection against deprivations of "liberty" without due process of law.

C) The penumbrae, or aura, surrounding several guarantees of the Bill of Rights.

D) The Tenth Amendment.

65. Assume that the City of Birmingham, Alabama, begins a program for minority set-asides for city contracting. Which of the following facts, if true, would be most useful in defending the program's constitutionality?

A) A city-conducted study had identified a history of discrimination against blacks in the building industry in Birmingham.

B) Congress had found in a nationwide study that black building contractors had been subject to extreme discrimination.

C) To be inclusive, the set-aside ordinance assisted contractors of every federally recognized racial minority, not just those that had been subject to past discrimination in Birmingham.

D) Birmingham had clear and precise evidence that minority contractors suffered disproportionately from financial hardships that made it difficult for them to get bonded, as required by standard contracting practice.

66. After the 2000 elections, the Alabama Legislature redraws the lines for its federal congressional districts. Which piece of evidence would be useful to a claim by a white voter that the state had unconstitutionally used race in drawing the district lines?

A) The district lines show no regard for local governmental units (i.e., the lines split up cities and counties and place pieces of them in different districts), but instead tend to group together similar socioeconomic groups (e.g., farmers and industrial workers).

B) The district lines show a careful regard for local government units; however, because cities and counties tend to be segregated, the effect of this attention to local government boundaries is to create racially homogenous districts.

C) The district lines deviate somewhat from a clean, geometrical pattern that had marked the results of the prior districting effort 10 years before.

D) None of these pieces of evidence would be enough to get a court to strictly scrutinize the districting lines.

67. Which of the following statements best describes the legal landscape after the Supreme Court's opinion in Marbury v. Madison?

A) The content of the Supreme Court's original jurisdiction was extremely fluid: Congress could give the Supreme Court original jurisdiction of any category of case as long as it fell somewhere within the federal judicial power.

B) The Court would not accept original jurisdiction over any case, as it is designed as an appellate court.

C) Any federal court had the power to declare a federal statute unconstitutional.

D) The Constitution was seen as document whose major provisions would have to be interpreted primarily by the political branches, with the ultimate check being the people's power to elect representatives who shared their view of the proper division of governmental powers.

68. Which of the following best describes the Ex Parte Young fiction?

A) It makes it possible for there to be a "case or controversy" for Article III purposes even though there is really only one party to the case.

B) It allows an individual to obtain an injunction against unconstitutional action by a state, despite the existence of the Eleventh Amendment.

C) It allows a case to be considered "ripe" for judicial decision even though the challenged statute has not yet been applied to the plaintiff.

D) It allows an individual to sue a state for damages despite the existence of the Eleventh Amendment.

69. Which of the following statements about standing is most accurate?

A) The Supreme Court's concern is solely that there be a "case or controversy" and that the court therefore have Article III authority to decide the case.

B) Standing speaks solely to the prudential concerns that might motivate a court to prefer not to decide a particular case or category of cases: it has nothing to do with Article III or any other constitutional requirements.

C) Standing speaks to both Article III and "prudential" concerns.

D) Standing is designed to ensure that both sides are, literally, "standing;" i.e., to ensure that the facts haven't changed so as to resolve the dispute that originally was the subject of the lawsuit.

70. Which of the following best describes Congress' control over the cases the Supreme Court can hear?

A) Congress may not withdraw jurisdiction from a case otherwise properly before the Supreme Court after the court has decided to hear the case.

B) Congress may withdraw jurisdiction from a case otherwise properly before the Supreme Court, but may not change the underlying substantive law in a way obviously meant to affect the decision in that case.

C) Congress may not withdraw the Supreme Court's jurisdiction from a case otherwise properly before that court, but it may withdraw the jurisdiction of a federal trial court to hear a case that has already been filed in that court, as long as the case has not yet proceeded to trial.

D) Congress may change the underlying substantive law governing a particular case already before a federal court, but it may not apply that change to a case if the judgment of a federal court in that case is already final.

Questions 71–73 refer to the following federal statute restricting abortion, enacted in 2009:

§1. No hospital or clinic receiving federal funds shall perform abortions during the last three months of a woman's pregnancy, unless the life of the mother is in imminent danger.

§2. Challenges to this statute, or to any state law regulating abortion, on the ground that this statute or the challenged state law violates the U.S. Constitution, shall be heard only by an Article III court entitled the "United States Abortion Court." This court shall be composed of a rotating panel of eleven judges chosen at random from current federal appellate judges. Decisions by this court shall be final. Specifically, no decision of this court shall be appealable to the United States Supreme Court.

§3. Any case challenging any state law described in §2 that is pending before any other federal court, including the United States Supreme Court, on the day that this bill becomes law, shall be immediately transferred to the United States Abortion Court. Such other federal court shall have no other power or jurisdiction with respect to such cases.

71. Is §2 constitutional?

A) **NO:** Claims that constitutional rights have been violated must be appealable to the Supreme Court.

B) **NO:** Because before 2009 Congress had vested the Supreme Court with appellate jurisdiction over cases in which a party was claiming violation of a constitutional right, it was without power in 2009 to strip such appellate jurisdiction, as the statute here attempts to do.

C) **YES:** Congress has complete power over federal jurisdiction; if it had wished, it could have prohibited any federal court from hearing a claim that an abortion restriction violated the Constitution.

D) **YES:** The United States Abortion Court is an Article III court.

72. Is §3 constitutional?

A) **NO:** Once a case is properly before the Supreme Court, Congress may not interfere by removing the Court's jurisdiction over the case.

B) **YES:** Congress can strip the Supreme Court of jurisdiction to decide a case even after the Court has heard oral argument and is deliberating.

C) **YES:** Congress can control the jurisdiction of the federal courts and prescribe the factual and legal conclusions a federal court must make.

D) **NO:** Because the United States Abortion Court is not mentioned in the Constitution, it is beyond Congress' power to vest it with any of "the judicial power of the United States."

73. Which of the following individuals could sue to challenge §1's ban on federal funding?

   I. An individual woman in the last three months of a pregnancy, alleging that she was now pregnant and wished to have an abortion in a hospital that received federal funds, and that she might become pregnant again.

   II. An individual woman in the last three months of pregnancy, suing on her behalf and on behalf of a class consisting of all women who would be pregnant during the pendency of the litigation.

   III. A doctor employed by a federally funded hospital, alleging that he would be unable to exercise his professional duty to his pregnant patients if he could not perform abortions during the last three months of pregnancy.

   IV. An association of California taxpayers which alleges that the statute would lead to a higher birth rate, thus requiring the state to spend more money on indigent pediatric care, requiring a higher level of state taxation.

   A) I and II.

   B) I, II, and III.

   C) I, II, and IV.

   D) II only.

Questions 74–76 deal with the following situation:

In 2009, after a remake of "Lassie" becomes the top-grossing file of all time, Congress enacts the "Take Our Pets to Work Act of 2009." The statute reads as follows:

§1. Any employer engaged in activity that affects interstate commerce shall make any reasonable accommodation to allow any employee to bring his or her pet to work.

§2. The requirements of §1 do not apply to exotic or potentially dangerous pets, or when a person's health or safety might reasonably be compromised by the presence of an animal in the workplace.

§3. The Secretary of Labor shall promulgate regulations to enforce this statute.

§4. Any regulations promulgated pursuant to §3 may be overturned by a two-thirds vote of both the Senate and the House of Representatives. Before any such vote, the House and Senate Labor Committees must report to their respective chambers, with a recommendation as to whether to overturn the regulation.

§5. Any employee, including an employee of a state or any instrumentality or arm thereof, claiming a violation of the Act may sue for damages and/or injunctive relief in federal or state court.

74. The Secretary of Labor promulgates a regulation stating that, under the "reasonable accommodation" standard, employers must provide and maintain litter boxes for any employee that brings a cat to work. Pursuant to §4, the House overturns the regulation. Is the House's action constitutional?

A) **YES**, as long as §4's procedures are complied with.

B) **NO:** The law delegates power to enforce the statute to the Secretary of Labor, who is a presidential appointee; any congressional oversight of the Secretary's actions would violate the separation of powers

C) **NO:** Such legislative action must satisfy the requirements of bicameralism and presentment

D) **YES**, because §4 requires a two-thirds vote, which is the proportion that enables Congress to act without the President (that is, to override a veto)

75. Sid Sidley is a dispatcher for the California Highway Patrol (CHP), and wishes to bring Precious, his Pekinese, to work. There is no exotic/dangerous pet or workplace safety problem, but the CHP still refuses to comply. Sid sues in state court, alleging that the CHP violated both the federal law and a state labor law requiring "fair and reasonable working conditions in every workplace in California." Sid's suit is eventually heard by the California Supreme Court, which holds that the CHP violated both the federal and the state law. The CHP appeals to the U.S. Supreme Court. What result?

A) Because of the important federalism implications raised by the federal law, the U.S. Supreme Court might decide to hear the case.

B) Because the state supreme court's decision rested on an adequate and independent state law ground, the U.S. Supreme Court would probably not hear the case.

C) Because the case started in state court, the U.S. Supreme Court would hold that it had no jurisdiction to hear the case.

D) Because of the respect for state court decisions mandated by Martin v. Hunter's Lessee, the U.S. Supreme Court would probably not hear the case.

76. Assume now that Sid sues in federal court, alleging violations of both the federal and state labor laws. On both claims Sid seeks both damages and injunctive relief. Which requests for relief would the court probably agree to consider?

  I. The request for damages based on state law.

  II. The request for an injunction based on state law.

  III. The request for damages based on federal law.

  IV. The request for an injunction based on federal law.

A) II, III, and IV.

B) IV only.

C) III and IV.

D) All of the above.

Questions 77–81 refer to the following fact pattern:

In 2009, after well-publicized outbreaks of E. coli poisoning, Congress enacts the "Pure Food Act Amendments of 2009." The statute reads as follows:

§1. Definitions: As used in this statute:
   1. "Commercial or institutional food server" shall include any entity, including non-profit organizations, states and state-owned entities, that habitually offer prepared food for sale to members of the public.

§2. Freshness: All commercial and institutional food servers shall use the most advanced technology reasonably available to ensure the freshness of all food intended to be sold or otherwise offered to any person.

§3. Fines: Any commercial or institutional food server found to have violated §2 shall be liable for a fine of up to $5,000 per day for every day there is a violation.

§4. Adjudication of Fines: Alleged violations of §3 shall be adjudicated in the first instance by Administrative Law Judges employed by the Department of Agriculture. Any party to such an adjudication may appeal any fact-finding or legal conclusion to any United States District Court where venue is proper. Said district court shall uphold any factual findings not held to be clearly erroneous, and shall review de novo any legal conclusions.

§5. Regulations: Regulations to implement this statute shall be promulgated by the Department of Agriculture. Challenges to said regulations shall be made to the United States District Court for the District of Columbia.

§6. Prohibitions on Sale: No commercial or institutional food server shall sell or otherwise serve food to any person if such seller or server has reason to know that such food may not be pure and wholesome.

§7. Private Party Recovery: Any person aggrieved by a commercial or institutional food server's violation of §6 shall be allowed to sue in federal court to recover any and all damages, including punitive damages as appropriate.

Sid Scowler, a student at a state-run law school in California, becomes ill after eating a tainted macro-wrap he purchased from the school-operated cafeteria.

77. Sid sues in federal court, naming as defendant the State of California and demanding damages as allowed by the statute. The State moves to dismiss. Which of the following best describes the probable result and rationale?

   A) The court would probably dismiss the case, because the statute already includes a remedial scheme.

   B) The court would probably **NOT** dismiss the case, because §1 of the statute reflects a clear congressional intent to hold states liable for damages.

C) The court would probably dismiss the case, because Congress cannot abrogate state sovereign immunity from suit in these circumstances.

D) The court would probably **NOT** dismiss the case, because Sid is suing the State under a validly enacted regulation of interstate commerce.

78. Assume now that Sid sues in federal court, naming the Dean of the Law School and the Chancellor of the University of California System as defendants, in their official capacities as Dean and Chancellor. In addition to the federal statutory violation, Sid alleges that the defendants violated their state law duty "to provide a safe educational environment for all public school students." Sid seeks damages for violation of federal law, and, on the state law count, an injunction mandating more regular inspection of the law school cafeteria. The defendants move to dismiss both counts. Which of the following best describes the probable result and rationale?

A) The court would probably dismiss both counts. The **FEDERAL** law count could not go on because, exceptions not relevant here, Congress cannot enact a statute making states liable for any relief that would require expenditures from the state treasury. The **STATE** law count could not go on either, because the Eleventh Amendment does not allow states to be sued in federal court on the basis of alleged violations of state law.

B) The court would probably let both counts go on. The **FEDERAL** law count could continue because Sid properly sued only state officials, while the **STATE** law count could go on because the Eleventh Amendment presents no bar to litigation of state law claims in federal court.

C) The court would probably let the **FEDERAL** law count go on, because the suit would be allowable under Ex Parte Young. However, the court would probably dismiss the **STATE** law count, because the Eleventh Amendment does not allow states to be sued in federal court on the basis of alleged violations of state law.

D) The court would probably dismiss the **FEDERAL** law count because Congress cannot abrogate state sovereign immunity from suit in these circumstances. However, the **STATE** law count could not go on either, because an injunction is the only thing being requested.

Questions 79–81 add the following facts to the above fact pattern:

The Department of Agriculture promulgates regulations under this statute prescribing that "the most advanced technology reasonably available," as that term is used in §2, requires use of a new, expensive, cryogenically based freezer technology that has come onto the market only in the last month. The American Restaurant Association (ARA) brings suit to enjoin enforcement of this regulation, arguing that the agency misunderstood what Congress meant by the term "reasonably available."

79. Under what circumstances would the ARA have standing bring this suit?

A) Only if the ARA itself operates a restaurant or is otherwise considered a food seller or server.

B) Only if one the ARA's members is considered a food seller or server, and only if that member is a named plaintiff in the suit.

C) Only if one of the ARA's members is considered a food seller or server, and only if the injunctive relief requested would not require the presence of the individual member as a named plaintiff in the lawsuit.

D) The ARA could not have standing.

80. Assuming the ARA has standing, which of the following best describes the route the court would take in deciding the merits of its claim?

A) Under Marbury, the court would review the statute de novo, giving no deference to the agency's interpretation of the statute.

B) The court would determine whether the statute provided a clear answer to the interpretive question; if not, the court would determine whether the agency's reading "in between the lines" of the statute was reasonable.

C) The court would uphold the agency's reading of the statute unless there was no rational basis at all for the agency interpretation.

D) The court would determine whether the statute provided a clear answer to the interpretive question; if not, the court would determine whether the agency's reading "in between the lines" of the statute was the best one.

81. The Agriculture Department brings an enforcement action against Leo's Luncheonette, alleging that the restaurant serves spoiled food. Leo's sues in federal court to enjoin the hearing before the Agriculture Department's Administrative Law Judge, arguing that such a hearing would violate the separation of powers. Which of the following statements is most accurate?

A) The right at issue is a private right, suggesting that the statute's hearing procedure is probably constitutional.

B) The fact that Article III courts could review the agency's fact-findings only under the deferential "clearly erroneous" standard strongly suggests that the statute's hearing procedure may be unconstitutional.

C) The statutory procedure is constitutional, because Article III imposes no limits on Congress' authority to provide for administrative adjudication of legal or factual issues, as long as the tribunal is a branch of the federal government.

D) The statutory procedure is probably constitutional, given the character of the right at issue and the reviewing role given to Article III courts.

82. In which of the following cases would the plaintiff have the best chance of establishing standing?

   A) A girl sues the public high school she attends, claiming that it deprived her of a university education by discriminatorily dropping girls' athletic programs; the plaintiff claims that had the school provided athletic programs for girls, she would have been a star and would have gotten an athletic scholarship to a university.

   B) A citizen of Miami sues the federal government under a provision of the Clean Water Act that allows "any person" to sue to correct violations of the statute; the plaintiff is a hydro-biologist with a professional interest in water purity, who claims that the government has consistently and egregiously failed to enforce the statute.

   C) A citizen of Miami sues the state of Florida, alleging that the state cut welfare funding in a manner violating the recipients' federal constitutional rights. The plaintiff never received welfare, but claimed that he operated a thrift store that catered to families on welfare; with the funding cut, his business has dropped substantially.

   D) An American citizen angry about the war in Iraq sues the federal government, claiming that it is mounting a war without a proper congressional declaration.

83. Which of the following statutes is most likely to be unconstitutional?

   A) A Texas law collecting a tax from grocery stores on all beef sold, the revenues from which are placed in a special account used to provide food assistance to poor families.

   B) A Texas law collecting a tax from grocery stores on all beef sold, the revenues from which are placed in the state's general revenue fund (i.e., the fund into which all tax money is normally placed); the law also provides that in-state cattle ranchers shall receive a subsidy of two cents for every pound of cattle they send to slaughter.

   C) A Texas law collecting a tax from grocery stores on all beef sold, the revenues from which are placed in a special account that funds a subsidy to in-state cattle ranchers of two cents for every pound of cattle they send to slaughter.

   D) A Texas law providing a subsidy to in-state cattle ranchers of two cents for every pound of cattle they send to slaughter, and establishing the "Texas Beef Board," an agency established "for the purpose of encouraging Texas consumers to 'switch to the taste of real Texas beef.'"

84. Which of the following statements about speech that incites a riot is true?

   A) For such speech to be punishable, the speaker need not have intended to cause illegal conduct, if the speech was likely to do so.

B) For such speech to be punishable, the speech need not have been objectively likely to cause illegal conduct, as long as the speaker intended that it do so.

C) For such speech to be punishable, the speaker had to have intended to cause illegal conduct, and such conduct had to have been a likely result of the speech.

D) Incitement speech is always protected as long as it addresses a topic of public interest or concern.

85. To what extent can Congress delegate legislative power to an administrative agency?

A) Congress can never delegate such power, and the Supreme Court has zealously enforced this requirement.

B) Congress may delegate to an agency the power to enact regulations, as long as Congress provides an "intelligible principle" to guide the agency's discretion.

C) Congress may delegate to an agency the power to enact regulations, but Congress must not provide overly detailed direction, lest it violate Article II's command that the Executive Branch execute the laws.

D) The Supreme Court has never struck down a statute as an unconstitutional delegation of legislative power.

Questions 86–91 relate to the following federal statute:

§1. Employment Discrimination:
No employer shall discriminate against any employee on the basis of sexual orientation.

§2. Definitions:
1. "Employer" means any natural person, state, federal or local government or any unit or subunit thereof, or corporation or partnership that employs any person.

§3. Enforcement:
a. On a first offense any offender shall be required to undergo diversity training not to exceed 16 hours in length, and to negotiate with the victim of the discrimination in order to rectify the discrimination to the satisfaction of both parties.
    If such negotiations do not succeed within 30 days, the federal district court in the district in which the discrimination occurred may order such negotiation under the sponsorship of a federal labor mediator.
b. On a second offense any offender shall pay a fine to the United States Treasury in the sum of the greater of $500 or the salary earned by the victim in one week.
c. On a third or any latter offense the victim may sue the employer for back pay and damages.

86. Can Sally bring a suit against the state employment director seeking an injunction against further discriminatory acts?

    A) **YES**, because this would be a straightforward application of Ex parte Young.

    B) **NO**, because Ex parte Young relief applies only to violations of state law.

    C) **NO**, because the statute includes a detailed remedial scheme.

    D) **YES**, as long as she first sought and gained the other relief provided for in the statute.

87. Which of the following constitutional provisions, if its/their conditions were satisfied, would authorize Congress to make states pay back-pay awards under this statute?

    I. The Commerce Clause

    II. The Ninth Amendment

    III. Section 5 of the Fourteenth Amendment

        A) I and II.

        B) I and III.

        C) I only.

        D) III only.

88. Which of the following statements is most accurate about Congress' authority to enact this statute under its power to enforce the Fourteenth Amendment?

    A) Because the statute benefits a non-suspect class, Congress would need to provide more evidentiary support for the statute than it would if the statute benefited a suspect class.

    B) Because the statute benefits a suspect class, Congress would need to provide more evidentiary support for the statute than it would if the statute benefited a non-suspect class.

    C) The suspectness of the benefited class is irrelevant to the amount of evidentiary support Congress has to provide for the statute.

    D) Congress does not need to provide actual evidence in support of §5 legislation, as long as the Supreme Court can perceive a rational basis for Congress' judgment.

89. Instead of suing based on the federal law, Sally sues under Illinois anti-discrimination law, which includes stronger anti-discrimination guarantees. Illinois defends by arguing that the federal statute preempted state law. Which of the following would best describe the court's response to the state's argument?

A) The lack of an explicit statement expressing Congress' desire to preempt state law means that the state law is not preempted.

B) The fact that the state and federal laws both address the same topic probably means that the state law is preempted, given the presumption of preemption grounded in the Constitution's Supremacy Clause.

C) The fact that the state and federal laws both address the same topic is irrelevant to preemption.

D) The fact that the state and federal laws both address the same topic might mean that the federal law preempts state law by occupying the field.

90. Which of the following is the best explanation for why §1 of the statute is constitutional?

A) Because the statute regulates an instrumentality of interstate commerce.

B) Because employment is an economic activity.

C) Because the statute's focus on equality makes it appropriate legislation to enforce the Fourteenth Amendment's Equal Protection Clause.

D) Because the Supreme Court recognized in Romer v. Evans that government action discriminating against gays and lesbians can sometimes violate the Equal Protection Clause.

91. Assume that Illinois defends against Sally's suit on the ground that the statute unconstitutionally commandeers state governments. How would a court rule on that argument?

A) It would **REJECT** that argument because the anti-commandeering doctrine does not apply when Congress is clearly regulating activities that substantially affect interstate commerce.

B) It would **REJECT** that argument because the statute does not "commandeer" state government, as the Supreme Court has used that term.

C) It would **REJECT** that argument because commandeering occurs only when the federal government attempts to regulate state law enforcement.

D) It would **REJECT** that argument because the statute envisages enforcement by federal courts; if the statute had required state courts to hear these claims then there would be unconstitutional commandeering.

92. Every December the City of St. Louis puts up a Christian nativity scene as part of its holiday directions on the City Hall lawn. It has put up such a scene every year since 1810, and, indeed, the pieces of the scene have developed historical value as mementoes of the city's early history. How would a court analyze the constitutionality of the city's action?

A) If the city combined secular and religious symbols of Christmas, a court would be less likely to uphold the display.

B) Intent is irrelevant to the analysis; as long as the action does not have "a clearly discernable religious impact," then the action is constitutional.

C) It would determine whether the city's action had the purpose or effect of advancing religion; if it does, then the city loses.

D) If the city combined secular and religious symbols of Christmas, the court's analysis would not be affected.

93. The State of Ohio decides to give cash grants to all private elementary schools in the state, based on each school's number of pupils. John Jones sues to have this expenditure declared unconstitutional as an establishment of religion. Does he have standing?

A) **NO**, because he is claiming a generalized grievance.

B) **YES:** Although normally this would be a generalized grievance, the Supreme Court has made an exception to this rule for Establishment Clause challenges to government expenditures in support of religion.

C) **YES:** The bar on generalized grievances does not apply to constitutional claims.

D) **YES**, but only if he can show that he lives near a private elementary school.

94. On December 30, the Washington Post uncovers from government sources knowledge of a terrorist plan to drop anthrax spores from an airplane flying over Manhattan on January 1. The Post plans to print the story on December 31, and the federal government seeks an emergency injunction against printing. What rule best governs how the court should rule?

A) Because prior restraints are almost never allowed, the government would bear a heavy burden in seeking to justify its request.

B) Because the government could easily punish the Post after the fact it if published the article, and because such punishment is the effective equivalent of a prior restraint, the government could obtain the injunction only by proving by a preponderance of the evidence that the information was illegally obtained.

C) As long as the court was a neutral decision-maker, the main concern behind the rule against prior restraints would be satisfied and the court would probably issue the injunction.

D) Because there is an absolute rule against prior restraints, the government could not obtain it.

95. Which of the following statements about the Contracts Clause is/are true?

I. It applies only against the States.

II. It was incorporated against the States via the Fourteenth Amendment.

III. It prevents interference with prospective contractual relations.

IV. It prevents interference with current contractual relations.

    A) I and III.

    B) I and IV.

    C) II and II.

    D) II and IV.

96. Which of the following statements about Congress' power to enforce the Fourteenth Amendment is/are correct?

I. The Amendment itself restricts only government action, but Congress, to enforce that restriction, may also regulate private parties.

II. The Amendment itself restricts only government action and the Supreme Court has held that Congress, to enforce it, may only regulate government actors.

III. The Amendment itself restricts only government action but the Supreme Court has never decided whether Congress, to enforce it, may regulate private parties.

IV. Congress can enforce the Amendment only by generalizing the particular results of cases decided by the Court, and by creating procedural and jurisdictional means for plaintiffs to vindicate the rights found by the Court.

    A) I and IV.

    B) II only.

    C) III only.

    D) III and IV.

97. The City of Richmond decides to revitalize part of its downtown by having private contractors build an arts and entertainment district consisting of theaters, galleries, and restaurants. To make the project a reality, it plans to use its power of eminent domain to take title to several parcels of land in that area, so it can re-sell them to the project developers. What is the owners' strongest constitutional claim against the project?

    A) Because the city plans to turn the land over to private developers, its actions violate the Takings Clause by not being for a public use.

B) Because the city is taking title to the property, it must pay just compensation.

C) The city may not take title to the land, regardless of whether it offers to pay compensation.

D) Because the city is transferring property from one party to another, it is violating the Equal Protection Clause.

98. Which of the following best describes the political-question doctrine?

A) It is a doctrine that deals with infringements on political rights, such as the right to vote and the right to hold elective office.

B) It is a doctrine that seeks to determine when a court has jurisdiction to hear a case that implicates the other branches of the federal government.

C) It is a doctrine that seeks to determine when a court should hear a case that implicates the other branches of the federal government, even if jurisdiction is otherwise proper.

D) It is a doctrine that arises when courts consider delicate issues of federalism.

99. Which of the following statements best describes the government's power to distinguish between citizens and non-citizens?

A) The federal government has substantially less discretion to distinguish between citizens and non-citizens than do states.

B) States have substantially less discretion to distinguish between citizens and non-citizens than does the federal government.

C) States and the federal government have the same discretion to distinguish between citizens and non-citizens.

D) Because immigration is a federal matter, states have no discretion to distinguish between citizens and non-citizens.

100. What is the constitutional status of libelous speech?

    I. As speech that often addresses public matters, it has full First Amendment protection.

    II. Libel itself has no First Amendment protection, but, to protect speakers from being chilled by the prospect of legal liability, the Supreme Court has insisted on strict burdens of proof for some libel claims.

    III. Libelous opinions are not protected, but libelous statements of fact are.

    IV. Libel is protected only if it addresses topics of public interest.

        A) IV only.

        B) II only.

C) II and IV.

D) I and III.

101. The Minneapolis School District has never been formally found guilty of seg-regating students by race; however, in 1977 it settled a lawsuit alleging that it had done so, without conceding guilt. Thirty-two years later, the School District wishes to use race as a factor in assigning students to kindergartens, to relieve the racial imbalance in the various kindergartens in the district that it believes its own conduct may have contributed to. To what extent may it do so?

A) It may do so subject only to lenient judicial scrutiny, given that its own illegal conduct was a cause of the current segregation.

B) It may do so only if a court finds that the district's belief in its own culpa-bility was reasonable.

C) Its decision to do so would be subject to strict scrutiny, as the District has not been formally judged guilty of segregation.

D) It may do so only at the kindergarten level, given the greater deference school districts have when dealing with small children.

102. Which of the following sources of congressional power authorizes Congress to make states liable for retrospective relief, such as damages?

I. The power to regulate interstate commerce.

II. The power to regulate commerce among the Indian tribes.

III. The power to enforce the Fourteenth Amendment.

IV. The power to enact bankruptcy laws.

A) III only.

B) III and IV.

C) I and II.

D) I and III.

103. Michael Rodriguez is a deputy district attorney for the County of Brunswick in the State of North Carolina. Part of his job is writing up recommended dis-positions for criminal misdemeanors. After he writes a recommendation that a particular misdemeanor not be prosecuted because the investigating officer fabricated evidence, he is disciplined. He sues, alleging violation of First Amendment rights. What result?

A) He loses, because the speech was made as part of his official duties.

B) He loses unless he can show that the speech was on a matter of public interest.

C) He loses unless he can show the content of the speech was true.

D) He wins unless the government can show that that the discipline was narrowly tailored to meet a compelling government interest.

104. What is the current status of the Second Amendment's right to bear arms?

A) The right protects only the right of citizens to bear arms as part of the militia.

B) The right includes the right of citizens to bear arms for self-defense, without any limitation as to where arms can be carried and by whom.

C) The right includes the right of citizens to bear arms for self-defense, but governments appear to retain the right to restrict the locations into which arms can be carried and whether they can be carried by felons and the mentally ill.

D) The right protects only the right of citizens to bear arms as part of the militia, but implies a government authority to restrict militia membership to exclude felons and the mentally ill.

105. Which of the following statements best describes the current status of the rights of students to free speech in schools?

A) The Court has overruled prior precedents and embraced the rule that schools have complete freedom to restrict student speech.

B) The Court has extended the rationale of prior precedents and made it even more difficult than before for schools to restrict student speech.

C) The Court has reaffirmed that students have First Amendment rights, but has allowed restrictions of that right for the purpose of deterring student use of drugs.

D) The Court has never drawn distinctions between students' speech rights and the speech rights of the general public.

106. State U.'s School of Law adopts an affirmative-action program that counts membership in a historically underrepresented minority group as a "plus" factor in an applicant's admissions file. A white applicant who was rejected and who did not receive the benefit of this "plus" factor sues, alleging racial discrimination. Which of the following statements best reflects how a court would likely analyze the claim?

A) The court would most likely defer to the School's judgment that the racial diversity encouraged by this policy assisted in the educational mission of the school.

B) Because this is a racial classification, the court would most likely examine closely the school's argument that the racial diversity encouraged by this policy assisted in the educational mission of the school.

C) Following Supreme Court precedent, the court would most likely reject any racial diversity justification for the policy, but it would be more receptive to a claim that the policy was designed to remedy general societal discrimination against those minority groups.

D) The court would probably uphold such a policy on either the diversity rationale or the societal discrimination rationale.

107. The federal government bans the cultivation and possession of marijuana. Sid Seeger grows his own marijuana from plants he found in the woods, using only rainwater to irrigate them. When arrested for violating the federal law he alleges that, as applied to him, the federal law exceeds federal regulatory power. What result?

A) Sid **WINS**: This is a rare case in which the activity is so completely local and unconnected to interstate commerce that Congress could not regulate it.

B) Sid **LOSES**: Congress has the power to legislate "for the general welfare," which would allow it to determine that marijuana possession of any type should be illegal.

C) Sid **LOSES**: Congress could rationally conclude that even marijuana grown and possessed in this manner could "leak out" into the interstate market and affect the federal government's attempts to stamp out the product.

D) Sid **WINS**, because the production and possession of marijuana is a local activity that is reserved to the states under the Tenth Amendment.

108. Assume the same federal statute as in the previous question. But now assume as well that the State of Oregon has a law that allows possession of small amounts of marijuana when prescribed by a doctor to alleviate pain. Tom Thompson suffers from cancer, and has a prescription to use marijuana. He grows the marijuana himself, using only rainwater as irrigation. Does the federal government have authority to prosecute his conduct?

A) No, because the state law immunizes his conduct.

B) No, normally the state law would not immunize his conduct from federal regulation, but the indirectness of the effects of Tom's conduct on interstate commerce suffices to do so.

C) Yes, as long as the federal government has a rational basis for believing that marijuana prescribed under the Oregon law will "leak out" into the interstate market.

D) Yes, as long as the federal government proves that marijuana prescribed under the Oregon law will "leak out" into the interstate market.

109. The Fraternal Order of Gophers, a men's social lodge active in Montana, gives the State of Montana a large stone tablet on which are inscribed the Ten Commandments. The State places the tablet on its capitol grounds, in a sculpture garden featuring sculptures highlighting the various groups of people who inhabit the state. A citizen sues, alleging the sculpture violates the Establishment Clause. Which of the following states most accurately how a court would analyze this issue?

A) The court would investigate whether the tablet contained a religious message: If it did, it would find an Establishment Clause violation.

B) The court would investigate whether the tablet was effectively the property of the state: if it was it would find an Establishment Clause violation because it contains a religious message.

C) The court would consider whether the tablet conveys a significant secular message, even if a religious message is necessarily also present; if it does, it would find no Establishment Clause violation.

D) The court would consider whether the tablet conveys an exclusively secular message; only in such a circumstance would it find no Establishment Clause violation.

110. After clashing with the town zoning board over an unrelated matter, Stella Stevens finds that the board has denied her a permit to expand her garage. She sues, alleging that the board has violated her equal protection rights, and claiming that the board approved similar requests made by her neighbors. What result?

A) Stella will probably lose, because equal protection claims can arise only when a plaintiff alleges discrimination based on her possession of a class-based trait, such as race or gender, and not based on her membership in a "class of one."

B) Stella could possibly win, though she would need to show that the zoning board treated her differently based on personal dislike or animus.

C) Stella could possibly win, though she would need to show that the zoning board had no rational basis for singling her out for differential treatment.

D) Stella will probably lose because discrimination with regard to trivial items such as building permits does not raise equal protection claims.

111. Assume instead that Stella was an employee at the zoning board. She is fired, and she alleges she was fired because she was singled out from all the employees in her office who were all performing at the same level. Could Stella prevail on her claim?

A) Possibly, if she could show that the government employer had no rational basis for choosing her as the one to be fired.

B) Possibly, but she would have to show that the government employer was motivated by personal dislike of Stella.

C) No, because equal protection claims can only arise when a plaintiff alleges discrimination based on her possession of a class-based trait, such as race or gender, and not based on her membership in a "class of one."

D) No, because the "class of one" theory does not apply in the government workplace.

112. The federal government taxes peach growers and uses the proceeds to mount an advertising campaign urging Americans to eat peaches. Larry LaSalle, a peach grower, sues the government, claiming that the program coerces him to fund speech with which he disagrees. Which of the following statements best describes the law governing his claim?

A) Citizens have no right to protest a specialized tax that funds a particular speech program.

B) Citizens may have a First Amendment right against a specialized tax that funds a particular speech program if the tax funds only the speech and is not part of a general marketing or production scheme.

C) Citizens may have a First Amendment right against a specialized tax that funds a particular speech program if a court concludes that the speech is the government's own.

D) Government may never tax citizens in order to fund government speech.

113. Which of the following statements best states the current law governing the First Amendment status of political campaign contributions?

A) Because money is not speech, government has complete latitude to restrict the amount of campaign contributions any individual may make.

B) A campaign contribution may signify an individual's support of a candidate; thus, restrictions on the amount of campaign contributions may be acceptable but a complete ban on contributions is not constitutional.

C) A campaign contribution may signify an individual's support of a candidate and the amount of the contribution may signify the intensity of the support; thus, government may not limit the amount of campaign contributions.

D) The federal government may limit campaign contributions, but state governments may not.

114. Which of the following statements most accurately states the law governing the Fourteenth Amendment's Privileges and Immunities Clause?

A) The clause protects a broad array of liberty interests.

B) The clause protects only a limited set of rights said to derive from "national citizenship."

C) The clause guarantees that states not discriminate unreasonably against out-of-staters.

D) The clause is the source of the rule that racial classifications enjoy "strict scrutiny."

115. Which of the following best states the law governing the size of state legislative districts?

A) Under the Equal Protection Clause state governments have complete power to structure their legislatures in any way they choose, including make some legislative districts significantly larger than others in terms of population.

B) State governments can only make districts in the upper house of the legislature significantly larger than other upper-house districts in terms of population; this rule allows state legislatures to parallel the United States Congress, where Senators represent states with vastly different populations.

C) State governments must make their legislative districts nearly equal in population in order to satisfy the requirements of the Equal Protection Clause.

D) The question of the size of state legislative districts is a political question that federal courts will not consider.

CONSTITUTIONAL LAW
MULTIPLE CHOICE
ANSWERS & ANALYSIS

> ## CONSTITUTIONAL LAW ANSWERS AND ANALYSIS

1. Issue: Legislative Veto

The correct answer is **C**. A legislative veto occurs any time Congress attempts to change the legal status of persons outside the legislative branch (i.e., legislates) through means less than full bicameralism and presentment. Section 5 clearly authorizes legislation short of presentment and thus is a legislative veto. A is incorrect, as it reflects the views of Justice White's dissent in INS v. Chadha (1983). B is also wrong; an agency regulation changes people's legal rights as much as a statute does, and at any rate congressional countermanding of that regulation would clearly be legislation under Chadha's definition. Finally, D is wrong because the fact that Congress might impose a legislative veto by a margin that would override a formal veto by the President (two-thirds of each house) doesn't cure the lack of presentment.

2. Issue: Non-Delegation Under the Commerce Clause

The correct answer is **C**. Item IV is the only correct answer component. Item I is incorrect; the Court's cases since the 1930s have made clear that this statute, in particular §3, provides an "intelligible principle" guiding the executive's discretion, and thus does not violate the non–delegation doctrine. Item II is also incorrect; the "anti-commandeering" doctrine applies only to federal commands to states, which are absent in this statute. Finally, item III is incorrect because the statute easily satisfies the Court's current requirements for valid Commerce Clause regulation. Internet transactions are clearly economic activities, which allows the Court to aggregate such transactions to determine whether they substantially affect interstate commerce. Given that the Court defers to congressional judgments in making such determinations, there's no serious question but that these transactions do have such an effect. But, as discussed in question 1, there is an unconstitutional legislative veto here. Thus, C, which reflects these conclusions, is the correct answer.

3. Issue: Preemption

The correct answer is **B**. A is incorrect because, while preemption is in fact concerned with federalism, it doesn't follow that the doctrine is inapplicable in state court; both state and federal courts have the authority to find state laws to be preempted. C is incorrect because it fails to take account of the presumption against preemption. Stating, as C does, that a court will find preemption "as long as the federal statute could reasonably be read as preempting," essentially reflects a presumption preemption, which is the exact opposite of the current law. D is incorrect because explicit statements of preemptive intention are not the only way to find preemption. B is correct, however. The only way that the state law might be thought to preempt would be if the state law somehow is thought to clash with federal regulatory objectives—there's no explicit preemptive statement in the federal law, it's physically possible to comply with both, and there's no indication that the federal law is intended to occupy the field. But it seems from the statute's findings that Congress is concerned with the security of online transactions, not fraud in general. Thus, there's no conflict between federal and state objectives.

4. Issue: Standing

The correct answer is **B.** A is incorrect because some standing requirements (injury, causation, and redressability) are constitutional in nature and thus cannot be bestowed by Congress. Note that Congress may be able to enact statutes that give individuals rights, the deprivation of which constitutes injury in the Article III standing sense, but Congress cannot simply direct that the Article III test is satisfied. C is incorrect because the Court has stated that injury may merely be imminent, and still be enough to constitute the kind of injury that would suffice for Article III standing. D is incorrect because, although the Court has recognized economic harm as a kind of injury sufficient for Article III standing purposes, it has also said that other types of harm would also suffice. B is correct because it reflects the Article III standing requirements of injury, causation, and redressability.

5. Issue: Article III Courts

The correct answer is **C.** Item III is the only correct answer component. Item I is wrong. The definition of private right has become more complex in recent decades, but even assuming the issue is a private right, that fact would counsel the statute's constitutionality, as the Court has always been more concerned with non–Article III federal tribunals hearing private right claims. II is incorrect because the nature of the right as private or public has always mattered to the Court. IV is incorrect because there has never been thought to be a constitutional right to have one's federal claims considered by more than one federal court. As long as the Internet Commerce Court is an Article III court—which it is, given its composition by Article III judges—that is all the Constitution requires. C is correct because it states the rule from Schor v. Commodities Futures Trading Corp. (1986) that a balancing test is appropriate to answer this type of question.

6. Issue: Retroactivity of Statutes and the Judicial Power

The correct answer is **D.** A is incorrect because the Court has upheld similar types of statutes, most notably in Robertson v. Seattle Audubon Ass'n (1992) against challenges that they violate the rule of United States v. Klein (1871). B is incorrect because Congress has substantial power to apply legal changes retroactively, subject only to a modest test for irrationality. C is correct, but not as complete as D. D is a better answer because it adds to C the idea that retroactive changes in the law cannot be made to apply to cases that have progressed to final judgment (Plaut v. Spendthrift Farm (1995)).

7. Issue: State Susceptibility to Federal Regulation

The correct answer is **C.** It states the rule from Garcia v. San Antonio Transportation Authority (1985), which overruled the contrary rule of National League of Cities v. Usery (1976). A is incorrect because under Garcia there is no bar to applying the statute's requirements to the states (as long as the plaintiff doesn't request damages against the state, in which case an Eleventh Amendment problem would arise under Seminole Tribe of Florida v. Florida (1996)); at any rate, the anti-commandeering doctrine would be the wrong federalism doctrine to invoke against the statute. B is incorrect because the statute is clearly authorized by the Commerce Clause, and any objection to Congress' use of that power in this case was rejected by Garcia. D is too broad; Congress cannot use its Commerce power to commandeer state legislatures or law enforcement (respectively, New York v. United States (1992) and Printz v. United States (1997)), even if it is regulating something that has a substantial effect on interstate commerce.

8. Issue: Congressional Power to Enforce the Fourteenth Amendment

The correct answer is **C.** The text of §5 gives Congress the power only to "enforce" the Amendment; thus A is incorrect. B is incorrect because, as noted in C, the Court has at times struck down statutes as going beyond Congress' §5 power. D is incorrect for the same reason, even though it correctly identifies the "congruence and proportionality" standard. C correctly states that standard and the results under it.

9. Issue: Separation of Powers

The correct answer is **D.** All of the other features are not problematic. A is incorrect because that is essentially the removal standard in the special prosecutor law that the Court upheld in Morrison v. Olsen (1988). B also reflects a feature in that law, which allowed a "Special Division" of Article III judges to appoint the special prosecutor, a feature the Court upheld in Morrison. C is incorrect because the power to remove a prosecutor for policy reasons is exactly the President argued for (unsuccessfully) in Morrison; although that case held that the President does not have that power as a matter of constitutional right, there is no problem with Congress giving him that power. D is constitutionally problematic, however, because it would give Congress direct control over the executive's power to prosecute legal violations — i.e., to execute the laws.

10. Issue: Interstate Commerce Power

The correct answer is **B.** The statute regulates an economic activity; therefore, United States v. Lopez's (1995) insistence on fact findings is irrelevant. That makes A incorrect. C is incorrect because under Garcia v. San Antonio Transit Authority (1985) Congress can regulate states' performance of economic activities under the Commerce Clause. D is incorrect because manufacturing itself is not commerce, but merely an activity that, at most, substantially affects interstate commerce. B is correct because manufacturing, an economic activity, will probably affect interstate commerce; at the very least the Court will defer to any congressional judgment that this particular activity, taken in the aggregate, does in fact affect interstate commerce.

11. Issue: Anti-Commandeering

The correct answer is **C**. Section 4 commandeers the state's law enforcement apparatus, by requiring it to conduct spot checks. But it does not commandeer the state legislature, because it doesn't require the legislature to do anything in particular with the information the sheriffs provide. Thus, B and D are incorrect. The correct answer is C, which correctly states this result. A is incorrect because, even though the statute regulates an economic activity that substantially affects interstate commerce, the Tenth Amendment's limits on federal powers prohibit the commandeering that §4 imposes.

12. Issue: Taxing Power

The correct answer is **C**. The Court decided in United States v. Butler (1936) that the taxing power is independent of Congress' regulatory power. Thus, A and B are both wrong. D is incorrect; although there is a general requirement of equality when laying taxes, it would not apply in this case.

13. Issue: State Sovereign Immunity

The correct answer is **D**. This question focuses on the Eleventh Amendment. Item I is wrong because under Seminole Tribe v. Florida (1996) the Interstate Commerce power doesn't authorize Congress to make states liable for retrospective relief such as damages. Item II is also wrong, because under Pennhurst Hospital v. Halderman (1985) Congress cannot make states liable under state law causes of action, regardless of the type of relief sought. For that reason, item III is wrong as well, making the correct answer D.

14. Issue: Dormant Commerce Clause

The correct answer is **C**. B is incorrect because it suggests that the Iowa law harms only out-of-state interests, which might make a court suspicious that it was an attempt to discriminate against interstate commerce. D is incorrect because the existence of an in-state pressure group in favor of the law doesn't mitigate any concern about discrimination against out-of-state interests. A is a close call, and in the absence of a better answer it might be correct, as it suggests a legitimate non-discriminatory reason for the bill. However, there may well be an ostensibly legitimate reason for a discriminatory statute. C suggests that in-state interests are harmed by the statute, which mitigates concern about intent to discriminate against interstate commerce. That makes C the best answer.

15. Issue: Dormant Commerce Clause

The correct answer is **B**. This question asks the exact opposite of the previous one. As indicated above, A and C tend to mitigate concern about discrimination against interstate commerce, which thus make them incorrect answers to this question. D helps the statute a little bit, by suggesting a legitimate reason for the statute, and so it too is incorrect. B suggests that no in-state group is harmed by the statute, which might lead to a court's being suspicious about the statute's discriminatory intent. For that reason it is the correct answer.

16. Issue: Dormant Commerce Clause

The correct answer is **C.** Item I is wrong because states cannot enter into reciprocity agreements that discriminate against certain states' commerce, even if the object is to entice the target states into adopting a more free trade policy. Item IV is wrong because Congress always has the power to allow or restrict state laws that discriminate against (or in favor of) interstate commerce. That reason also makes items II and III correct.

17. Issue: Equal Protection Scrutiny

The correct answer is **D.** The Court purports to adhere to a three-tiered scrutiny scheme, with race and national origin classifications getting strict scrutiny, gender and legitimacy getting intermediate scrutiny, and all other classifications getting rational basis. But in practice the Court has engaged in a much more nuanced approach that results in some rational basis classifications getting struck down (e.g., City of Cleburne v. Cleburne Living Center (1985)) and some strict scrutiny classifications getting upheld (e.g., Grutter v. Bollinger (2003)). D captures this reality.

18. Issue: State Action

The correct answer is **B.** Item I is incorrect because the Court has held that the fact that a contractor does most of its business for a state doesn't by itself make it a state actor. Instead, the Court focuses on the extent to which the challenged action is attributable to the state. Given that focus, II is wrong, because the contractor's gender discrimination is not related to the state's insurance requirements. However, the state's training requirements are closely related to the contractor's gender discrimination, which pertains exactly to that function. Thus, item III is correct.

19. Issue: Gender Classification Under Equal Protection

The correct answer is **C.** A and B misstate the appropriate scrutiny standard; officially, gender does not get strict scrutiny as suggested by A, whereas B understates the degree of fit and importance of the interest that would be required for the discrimination to survive judicial scrutiny. D is incorrect because the Court has made it clear that if an action perpetuates gender stereotypes then it is constitutionally problematic. D does that, by shunting women into traditional female job roles. That rationale also makes C the correct answer.

20. Issue: First Amendment Limits on the Regulation of Obscenity

The correct answer is **D.** The Miller standard for obscenity requires, among other things, that a jury find that the work, judged by community standards, appeals to prurient interest, displays sexual conduct in a patently offensive way, and, taken as a whole, is without serious artistic or other merit. This standard makes A and B incorrect, given that the facts tell you that the book has serious merit; that same analysis strongly suggests that D is correct. C is incorrect because obscenity is deemed to be beyond the protection of the First Amendment (Roth v. United States (1957)).

21. Issue: Incorporation Under the Contracts Clause

The correct answer is **C.** Item I is the Contracts Clause, which applies only against the states. The other items are parts of the Bill of Rights, most but not all of which have been held to apply to the states. In particular, the civil jury trial right and the right to an indictment before being subject to a criminal trial have not been incorporated to apply against the state. C reflects this.

22. Issue: Intent Requirement of Equal Protection Clause

The correct answer is **C.** This question deals with the intent requirement the Court has found in the Equal Protection Clause (Washington v. Davis (1976) and Village of Arlington Hts. v. Metro. Housing Dev. Corp. (1977)). For a classification such as gender to be considered as deserving of heightened scrutiny, the Court must conclude that the classification was intentional. To show this, the rule is that the plaintiff must show that an intent to classify on that basis was one of the motivators of the government's action. If the plaintiff shows that, then the defendant must prove that, despite the discriminatory intent, other factors mean that the government would have taken that same action, even absent the discriminatory intent- (Arlington Hts.). This rule is reflected in answer C.

23. Issue: Congressional Authority to Enforce the Fourteenth Amendment

The correct answer is **C.** The Court has suggested that Congress may abrogate the intent requirement under its §5 power (Tennessee v. Lane (2004); Washington v. Davis (1976)); thus I is wrong. The §5 power by definition allows Congress to regulate the conduct of state governments; thus III is wrong. IV is wrong in that it is too limited; Arlington Hts. indicates that courts may consider historical evidence of discrimination when deciding the defendant's intent. II is correct, because objective indicators can be used in determining intent, per Arlington Hts.

24. Issue: First Amendment Libel Standards

The correct answer is **A.** Under Gertz v. Robert Welch (1974), Catherine would not be a public figure. Thus, D is incorrect, since that states the rule for public officials. Instead, as a private figure suing on a matter of public interest (which this clearly is), A states the proper rule for punitive damages. That automatically makes C incorrect. B is incorrect because Gertz sets the proof requirements for punitive damages for a plaintiff in this situation.

25. Issue: Procedural Due Process

The correct answer is **D**. The rule, from Roth v. Bd. of Regents (1972), is that for someone to have a property interest protected by procedural due process, he must have a legally created expectation interest. The importance of the right (choice A) and his likely entitlement to the benefit (choices B and C) are irrelevant to that inquiry. D establishes his legal entitlement if he meets the criteria, and thus creates the property interest. For that reason it is the correct answer.

26. Issue: Procedural Due Process

The correct answer is **B**. The rule about how much process is due, from Mathews v. Eldridge (1976), is that the court should take into account the importance of the benefit to the class of recipients, the government's interest in denying the extra process, and the likelihood that the extra process will improve the accuracy of the government's decision. The only answer choice relevant to any of those factors is B, which speaks to the last of these factors. A is wrong because it speaks to John as an individual, not to the importance of the benefit to the entire class of beneficiaries. C and D are completely irrelevant to this inquiry.

27. Issue: Procedural Due Process

The correct answer is **B**. A is wrong because the termination and appeals procedures have nothing to do with the question whether John has a property interest, which is a distinct inquiry. C is wrong because Congress cannot control the due process inquiry by setting forth the procedures it chooses to provide; the question of what the Constitution requires is decided by the courts. D is wrong because the Due Process Clause itself does not create property interests. B is correct because it states the opposite of choice A, which, as explained above, is incorrect.

28. Issue: First Amendment Level of Scrutiny

The correct answer is **C**. In Pacifica v. FCC (1978) the Court held that the invasiveness of radio broadcasts justified more, not less, regulation; thus A is incorrect. B indicates some of the factors a court would examine when deciding on the correct review standard in a case like this, but its conclusion conflicts with the Court's decision in Turner Broadcasting v. FCC (1994), which announced that intermediate scrutiny was appropriate for this type of statute. D is incorrect, because outside the limited exception of campaign finance, the Court has never adopted the idea that one group's First Amendment rights can be sacrificed in order to ensure more discussion of core political issues. C correctly states the rule from Turner Broadcasting.

29. Issue: Equal Protection Challenge to Affirmative Action

The correct answer is **B**. A is incorrect because Bakke turned on the unique situation of higher education, and thus is irrelevant. C is incorrect because even in cases such as J.A. Croson v. Richmond (1989), the Court insisted that strict scrutiny does not mean fatal scrutiny. D is incorrect because in Adarand v. Pena (1995), the Court struck down a federal spending program that had a contracting set-aside. B is correct because the fact-findings in the question mirror the ones the Court found insufficiently precise in Croson.

30. Issue: Equal Protection Challenge to School Desegregation

The correct answer is **A**. In Swann v. Charlotte Bd. of Education (1971) the Court set forth a variety of remedial steps a court could order to ensure desegregation. That list included the remedy noted in A. The other remedies have been explicitly rejected in other cases: B and D were rejected in Missouri v. Jenkins (1995) and C was rejected in Freeman v. Pitts (1992).

31. Issue: Substantive Due Process

The correct answer is **A**. In Casey (1992) the Court found fault in Roe v. Wade's (1973) failure to value the state's interest in the potentiality of fetal life from the start of conception; thus, it allowed more regulation of early abortion decisions, as long as the woman retained the ultimate choice, until viability, at which time the state could ban abortion as long as it retained an exception for maternal health. Because the woman had to retain the ultimate choice until viability, B is incorrect. Because the state could ban late-term abortions, C is incorrect. Casey, not Roe, introduced the "undue burden" test; thus, D is incorrect.

32. Issue: First Amendment Forum Analysis

The correct answer is **B**. Only item IV is correct; therefore, B is the correct answer. I is wrong because content-based restrictions in public forums require more than simple reasonableness. II is incorrect because viewpoint-based restrictions are generally not allowed in public or non-public forums. III is incorrect because speech on private property gets the same protection as speech in a public forum. IV is correct; although content-based restrictions in public forums require something akin to strict scrutiny, if the forum is non-public then more relaxed rules apply.

33. Issue: Commercial Speech Under First Amendment

The correct answer is **D**. Even though the Court has been increasing the amount of protection such speech enjoys, ostensibly it still occupies a mid-range position of protection, less than that enjoyed by core political speech; thus A and B are incorrect. C is incorrect; this might have been the rule under the Posadas of Puerto Rico v. Tourism Co. (1986), but this has been repudiated more recently. D is correct, as it states the current rule from Central Hudson v. Public Serv. Commn. (1980).

34. Issue: Substantive Due Process

The correct answer is **B**. A is incorrect because the Court has grounded protection for family relationships in the Due Process Clause, not in the penumbras from enumerated rights, at least since Roe v. Wade (1973). C is incorrect because protection for these rights resurfaced in Griswold v. Connecticut (1965) and has continued to the present. D is incorrect for the same reason.

35. Issue: Equal Protection Challenge to Election Districting

The correct answer is **C**. The Court, in a series of cases starting with Shaw v. Reno (1993) has expressed concern with racial gerrymandering to increase minority representation; thus, D is incorrect. The three remaining choices deal with the standard for determining when there is in fact a racial gerrymander that justifies heightened scrutiny. Of these, C states the correct standard from one of these cases, Miller v. Johnson (1995).

36. Issue: First Amendment Establishment Clause

The correct answer is **A**. I is incorrect because the test from Lemon v. Kurtzman (1973) has been notably unsuccessful in yielding predictable results. II is incorrect because the Court has in fact showed great concern about promotion of religion generally over non-religion. IV is incorrect because Lemon asks, as one of its prongs, what the predominant effect of the challenged law was; thus, intent is not dispositive. III reflects the highly contextualized decision-making of the Court's cases dealing with nativity scenes and other religious displays on public property, such as in Allegheny County v. ACLU (1989) and McCreary County v. ACLU (2005).

37. Issue: First Amendment Associational Rights

The correct answer is **B**. A is incorrect as it represents the approach suggested by Justice O'Connor's concurrence in Roberts v. Jaycees (1984), which is not the majority view. C is incorrect because it is not content-based in the traditional sense; having a place of public accommodations is not formal speech that has content. Instead, the proper question is whether the statute violates the right to associate. D is incorrect because the right to association extends to expressive associations as much as intimate ones. B is correct, as it reflects the analysis in Roberts.

38. Issue: Takings

The correct answer is **D**. This question deals with the constitutionality of conditional development permits under Nollan v. Calif. Coastal Comm'n (1987) and Dolan v. Tigard (1994). A is incorrect because Dolan required heightened proportionality review when a development permit condition would constitute a taking if simply imposed, as this one would. B is incorrect; the 100% loss rule is from Lucas v. South Carolina Coastal Comm'n (1992) which is not a permit case. C is incorrect because that rule, like B, is based on standard takings analysis, not conditional permit analysis. D correctly states the Dolan rule.

39. Issue: Time, Place, and Manner Analysis Under the First Amendment

The correct answer is **C**. A is incorrect; speech on private property is protected as much as speech in a public forum, which requires more than viewpoint neutrality. B is incorrect because music is speech, under Ward v. Rock Against Racism (1989). D is incorrect because under Ward the Court would find this to be a content-neutral restriction, which would require less than strict scrutiny. For the same reason, C is the correct answer.

40. Issue: First Amendment Limits on the Regulation of Fighting Words

The correct answer is **B.** A is incorrect because the fighting-words doctrine has never been overruled. C is incorrect because wearing a jacket with a verbal message can constitute speech, as it did in Cohen v. California (1971). D is incorrect because B is the better answer. B is the better answer because the fighting-words doctrine from Cohen requires that there in fact be a threat of a violent reaction by listeners (or in this case, readers).

41. Issue: Forum Analysis

The correct answer is **C.** A is incorrect because the Court has not generally held that government owned property is a public forum. Some of it is, but much of it isn't. B and D are incorrect because they contradict C, which states the correct rule from Int'l Society for Krishna Consciousness v. Lee (1992).

42. Issue: First Amendment Free Exercise Clause

The correct answer is **D.** A is wrong; current Free Exercise doctrine protects belief and conduct, although protection for conduct may be relatively limited. B is incorrect because the Court has shied away from making judgments about the centrality of a particular practice to a given religion. C is incorrect; under Employment Division v. Smith (1990), generally applicable laws that happen to burden religion usually don't get strict scrutiny. D is correct because, like in Church of the Babalu v. Hialeah (1993), the statute seems to intentionally target religious practice, and thus under Hialeah it gets strict scrutiny.

43. Issue: Clear and Present Danger Doctrine

The correct answer is **B.** The question here is the proper standard for speech that presents a clear and present danger of unlawful conduct. Under Brandenburg v. Ohio (1969), such speech must be intended to result in illegal conduct AND be likely to succeed in doing so. This disqualifies choices C and D. As between A and B, the rhetorical nature of the speech, when combined with the Court's speech-protective application of Brandenburg, means that B is the better choice.

44. Issue: First Amendment Limits on the Regulation of Fighting Words

The correct answer is **D.** I is correct because, under Cohen v. California (1971), fighting words must present a direct threat of a violent reaction, which mere denigrating speech may not. II is correct because it singles out speech based on certain topics (e.g., race) for special treatment (see R.A.V. v. St. Paul (1992)). III is incorrect, because intent plays no role in this analysis. IV is incorrect, for the reasons given in the explanation of item II.

45. Issue: First Amendment Limits on the Regulation of Fighting Words

The correct answer is **A.** This choice states the rule from Wisconsin v. Mitchell (1993). Mitchell explicitly rejected the analysis in B, thus it, as well as C and D as well, are incorrect, as they all assume that the statute targets expression or thought.

46. Issue: Social and Economic Regulation Under Equal Protection Clause

The correct answer is **B.** This choice states the correct standard for rational-basis review of social and economic legislation under the Equal Protection Clause. A is incorrect because, although the Fourteenth Amendment doesn't apply to the federal government, the Fifth Amendment, which does, has been found to include an equality component (Bolling v. Sharpe (1955)). C is incorrect; recourse to the common law as the baseline for the appropriateness of statutory classifications was repudiated during the New Deal era. D is incorrect because it uses the wrong standard, taken from racial gerrymandering cases.

47. Issue: Substantive Due Process

The correct answer is **D.** A non-fundamental right would receive only rational basis review under due process, and thus would probably be upheld. The Court has never held that the Due Process Clause provides no protection at all for the right to contract; thus A is incorrect. B is incorrect because it states an incorrectly strict standard. C is incorrect because the Contracts Clause deals with impairments of existing contracts, not the right to bargain in the future.

48. Issue: Article IV's Privileges and Immunities Clause

The correct answer is **C.** None of the items is correct. I is incorrect, because most likely the right to buy home heating oil is not "fundamental" for purposes of the Privileges and Immunities Clause (see Baldwin v. Fish and Game Comm'n (1978)). II and III are incorrect because most likely the state's action in building the refinery and selling its product would come within the market participant exception to the Dormant Commerce Clause (see Reeves v. Stake (1980)).

49. Issue: Article IV's Privileges and Immunities Clause

The correct answer is **A.** I is correct under Paul v. Virginia (1868). II is correct under Baldwin v. Fish and Game Comm'n (1978), while that same case rejects the principle in (III). (IV) is incorrect; both of these clauses apply to the states.

50. Issue: Anti-Commandeering

The correct answer is **C.** This choice states the rule from Testa v. Katt (1947). A is incorrect because Article III would allow lower federal courts to have jurisdiction over such cases. B is incorrect, as the anti-commandeering doctrine has stopped short of stopping Congress from taking this sort of action (see Printz v. U.S. (1997), which reaffirmed Testa). D is incorrect, given Testa.

51. Issue: Interstate Commerce Power

The correct answer is **C**. A is incorrect as Seminole Tribe v. Florida (1996) doesn't allow Congress to enact legislation under the Commerce Clause making nonconsenting states liable for retrospective relief in federal courts. B is incorrect because state officers may be sued in federal court under Ex parte Young (1908). D is incorrect because Sam could sue a state official in federal court as well, again under Young. C correctly states the Young rule, which allows a suit against an official either in federal court or state court (see Alden v. Maine (1999)).

52. Issue: Interstate Commerce Power

The correct answer is **D**. Under Garcia v. San Antonio Trans. Authority (1985), the Court allows Congress to regulate states in their capacity as economic actors—e.g., as employers, polluters, or cable T.V. providers. Garcia overruled National League of Cities v. Usery (1976), which restricted congressional power to regulate "traditional state functions." Because Garcia is the modern rule, A and B are incorrect. C is incorrect also because Garcia didn't mention a balancing test. D states the rule from Garcia and thus is correct.

53. Issue: Legislative Veto

The correct answer is **C**. There is an unconstitutional legislative veto under INS v. Chadha (1983) because there is no presentment to the President. Mere presentment of the underlying bill isn't enough; thus, B is incorrect. A is incorrect; there is no bicameralism problem because under the law the congressional override of the regulation must go through both houses. D is incorrect because Congress can override an agency regulation, as long as it does so through a bill that satisfies bicameralism and presentment.

54. Issue: Incorporation

The correct answer is **B**. As of 2009, the Second Amendment has not been incorporated against the states (Presser v. Illinois (1886)). A is incorrect, as government compulsion of private action would make that private action imputable to the government. C is incorrect because the rational-basis standard would not require the government to prove anything, as the burden of proof would be on the plaintiff. D is incorrect because the Supreme Court has generally recognized that chattel can be heavily regulated without running afoul of the Takings Clause. Note that the answer to this question may be subject to change in subsequent cases.

55. Issue: Substantive Due Process and Equal Protection

The correct answer is **B**. This choice states the rule that the rational-basis standard of equal protection, which is what would apply here, requires the plaintiff to prove the lack of a classification's rationality. Thus, A is incorrect, as it reverses the burden of proof. C is incorrect because as of 2009, for Due Process purposes, owning a gun is not a fundamental right. D is incorrect because the common law no longer functions as the baseline against which to measure the appropriateness of government classification decisions.

56. Issue: Equal Protection Challenge to School Desegregation

The correct answer is **C**. This choice states the rule from Keyes v. School Dist. No. 1 (1973), which requires, in the absence of an official discrimination policy, a showing of some intent to segregate before a school district will be required to desegregate. A is incorrect because Ana could still win the suit if she makes this showing. B is incorrect because segregative effect, as opposed to intent, is insufficient. D is incorrect because legislative history, although relevant, is not the only tool a plaintiff can use to show segregative intent.

57. Issue: Judicial Remedies for School Segregation

The correct answer is **C**. The Supreme Court has held that courts may order a wide variety of actions to remedy school segregation, including pupil reassignment and bussing. But it has also held in cases such as Miliken v. Bradley (1974) that non-offending districts may not be brought into the court's remedial order. C states this combination.

58. Issue: Incorporation

The correct answer is **C**. The Court has incorporated the Speech, Cruel and Unusual Punishment, and Takings Clauses, but has never decided on the incorporation of the Excessive Fines Clause.

59. Issue: State Action

The correct is **C**. A is incorrect because the Court has severely limited the reach of the "public function" branch of the state action doctrine. B is incorrect because, while the city presumably gets some benefit from the existence of a bus company, the relationship is not as symbiotic as in cases where such a theory has prevailed, most notably, Burton v. Wilmington Parking Authority (1961). D is incorrect because the act of issuing I.D. cards for senior citizens by itself doesn't strongly suggest state support for the FTC's discrimination (although this may be the second best answer if the cards were issued in part to identify people by ethnicity—however, the facts indicate that only senior citizens, not all bus riders, got the cards). C is the best answer because of the tight degree of interconnection between the FTC and the city, which might lead individuals to associate the FTC in general with the city.

60. Issue: Gender Classification Under Equal Protection

The correct answer is **D**. A is incorrect because the Court continues to reserve the highest level of scrutiny for racial and ethnic classifications, and had explicitly stated that it is willing to accept classifications that either respond to real gender differences or compensate women for past discrimination. B is incorrect for the same reason, and also because classifications benefiting women do not get mere rational-basis review, but instead get some level of heightened scrutiny, to ensure that they're not simply perpetuating stereotypes under the guise of assisting women. C is incorrect because the Court has explicitly elevated gender to a higher level of scrutiny than social and economic regulation (Craig v. Boren (1976)). D is correct because it states the more permissive (though not necessarily rational-basis reviewed) status of legislation compensating women for past discrimination (United States v. Virginia (1996)).

61. Issue: Sexual Orientation Classification Under Equal Protection

The correct answer is **D.** In Romer v. Evans (1996) the Court struck down a sexual orientation classification even though it never held that such classifications get heightened review. Thus, A and B are incorrect. C is incorrect because in Lawrence v. Texas (2003) the Court struck down a statute prohibiting same-sex sexual conduct, as violating the liberty interests of those persons who engage in that conduct.

62. Issue: Incorporation

The correct answer is **C.** The Bill of Rights per se does not apply to state governments (Barron v. Baltimore (1835)); thus, A is incorrect. B is incorrect because the Fourteenth Amendment's incorporation of much of the Bill of Rights is not explicit, but has been accomplished as an interpretation of the Due Process Clause. D is incorrect because that process of interpretation has not resulted in every Bill of Rights guarantee being incorporated. C states the correct rule.

63. Issue: Incorporation

The correct answer is **C.** Item I applies against the states through the literal terms of the Due Process Clause of the Fourteenth Amendment. The rights in items II and III have not been incorporated, and thus do not apply to the states. Item IV restates the Contracts Clause, which applies to the states on its own force. Answer choice C reflects this combination.

64. Issue: Sources for Individual Rights

The correct answer is **D.** All the other provisions have been used by Justices as sources for the rights underlying cases such Griswold and Roe. The Tenth Amendment, a federalism provision, is not relevant to those rights and thus is the correct answer.

65. Issue: Equal Protection Challenge to Affirmative Action

The correct answer is **A.** In cases such as Croson v. Richmond (1989), the Supreme Court has insisted that affirmative action set-asides be justified by precisely relevant evidence documenting the discrimination the set-aside sought to remedy. B is incorrect because nationwide evidence is considered too general to justify a locality's set-aside. C is incorrect because it suggests that the city's program would be broader than necessary to remedy the discrimination at which the plan was aimed. D is incorrect because financial hardships don't directly relate to racial discrimination, and at any rate that disparity could be combated by a non-race conscious remedy. A is correct because it suggests evidence precise both to the locality and the particular industry to which the set-aside applies.

66. Issue: Equal Protection Challenge to Election Districting
The correct answer is **D.** The Court has stated that for such line-drawing to be strictly scrutinized as a race classification, the predominant motivating factor had to have been race. None of the answer choices reflects this. The Court has accepted grouping voters based on socioeconomic or other factors as well as the relevance of city and county lines. Thus, A and B are incorrect. The Court has stated that "bizarrely shaped" districts may be subject to higher scrutiny, but the facts of C don't suggest that the lines rise to the level of bizarreness.

67. Issue: Judicial Review
The correct answer is **C.** The Court gave a narrow reading to Article III's grant of original jurisdiction to the Supreme Court, thus A is incorrect. B is incorrect because the Court in Marbury never stated that it would not accept a grant of original jurisdiction that was consistent with Article III. D is incorrect because the Court in Marbury established that courts have the power of judicial review. C is correct because that power, described in Marbury as an incident to deciding a case, logically would flow to any federal court with the authority to decide a case.

68. Issue: State Sovereign Immunity
The correct answer is **B.** Young deals with sovereign immunity; thus, A and C are incorrect. D is incorrect because Young suits cannot seek retrospective relief such as damages, but only forward-looking relief, such as injunctions (Edelman v. Jordan (1974)). This makes B correct.

69. Issue: Standing
The correct answer is **C.** Standing speaks to both prudential and constitutional concerns; thus, A and B are incorrect. D is incorrect, as it describes the mootness, not the standing, requirement.

70. Issue: Article III Jurisdiction
The correct answer is **D.** Congress may withdraw a court's jurisdiction to hear a case at any time before final judgment, and may change the substantive law the court must apply. But it must not disturb a final judgment (Plaut v. Spendthrift Farm (1995)).

71. Issue: Article III Jurisdiction
The correct answer is **D.** Answer A is incorrect because the Supreme Court has never held that there is a constitutional right to appeal a decision to it. Answer B is incorrect because Congress has power to strip the Supreme Court's jurisdiction as well as to grant it (Ex parte McCardle (1868)), subject to potential

limitations that are not implicated by these facts. Answer C is close, but because there may potentially be limits on Congress' power to entirely strip the federal courts of jurisdiction over a given class of cases, it is wrong. D states the correct rule; allowing a claim to be heard in at least one Article III court is an important consideration in deciding whether Congress has acted unconstitutionally in limiting federal jurisdiction.

72. Issue: Article III Jurisdiction

The correct answer is **B.** This choice states the rule from Ex parte McCardle (1868). A is incorrect because it conflicts with the result in McCardle. C is incorrect because the prescribing of factual findings and legal conclusions might run afoul of United States v. Klein (1871). D is incorrect because the abortion court is an Article III court; there is no requirement that such a court be explicitly mentioned in the Constitution (indeed, aside from the Supreme Court, no particular federal court is explicitly mentioned).

73. Issue: Standing

The correct answer is **B.** I is a correct response, as it reflects a situation in which the plaintiff has standing, and in which mootness would not be a problem, because her condition is capable of repetition but evading review (Linda R.S. v. Richard D. (1973)). II is also correct, because a class action also takes care of any mootness problems. III is also correct, as it reflects a situation where the Court has found third party standing to be appropriate (Singleton v. Wulff (1976)). IV is not correct, as it reflects a situation where the Court has found third–party standing not to be appropriate (Warth v. Seldin (1974)). Thus, I, II, and III are the correct responses, which makes B the correct answer choice.

74. Issue: Legislative Veto

The correct answer is **C.** That section constitutes a legislative veto, which is unconstitutional under INS v. Chadha (1983). All legislative action affecting the rights of people outside of Congress requires both bicameralism and pre-sentment; §4 lacks presentment. A is therefore incorrect, as is D. B is incorrect because Congress may engage in oversight of agency action, and may overturn an agency regulation, as long as it does it by means of a full-blown statute.

75. Issue: Adequate and Independent State Law Ground

The correct answer is **B.** Because the judgment in Sid's favor would remain even if he lost at the Supreme Court on the federal claim, it would rest on an adequate and independent state law ground, and thus would not be reviewed by the Supreme Court. A is incorrect because the appeal would not present a case or controversy and thus the court would not hear it. C is incorrect because there is no jurisdictional rule against the Supreme Court hearing a case on appeal from a state court (see Martin v. Hunter's Lessee (1816)). D is incorrect because, if anything, Martin counsels in favor of the Supreme Court's power to hear appeals from state courts.

76. Issue: State Sovereign Immunity

The correct answer is **B.** Only an injunction based on federal law, based on Ex parte Young (1908), would be available. Damages based on federal law are not allowed, under Seminole Tribe v. Florida (1996), unless the statute was based on the Fourteenth Amendment or the Article I bankruptcy power, which this one is clearly not. No relief based on state law is allowed (Pennhurst v. Halderman (1985)). Thus, only item (IV) is correct, which makes B the correct answer.

77. Issue: State Sovereign Immunity

The correct answer is **C.** A is incorrect because the existence of a detailed remedial scheme defeats the applicability of a Young suit seeking an injunction, not a damages suit that seeks the damages provided in the statute. B is incorrect because congressional intent to abrogate is not enough to make the abrogation effective; Congress must also have a constitutional basis for doing so. D is incorrect because it assumes that the statute is valid, when in fact it violates the rule in Seminole Tribe v. Florida (1996) that Article I doesn't authorize Congress to make states liable for retrospective relief. C states the correct rule.

78. Issue: State Sovereign Immunity

The correct answer is **A.** The federal suit could not go forward because in a case like this, where Congress is legislating under its commerce authority, it cannot make states liable for retrospective relief such as damages (Seminole Tribe v. Florida (1996)). The state suit could not go forward because under Pennhurst v. Halderman (1985) the Eleventh Amendment does not allow state law–based claims against non-consenting states. For these reasons, B and D are incorrect. C is incorrect because a suit seeking damages is not a proper Ex parte Young suit.

79. Issue: Standing

The correct answer is **C.** An association may sue in lieu of one its members as long as one member would have standing in its own right, the interest the association is asserting is germane to the reason for the association's existence, and the relief would be effective in the absence of the individual members (Warth v. Seldin (1974)). Thus, A is incorrect because the ARA need not have standing on its own. B is incorrect because it is not necessary that the individual member be a named plaintiff. D is incorrect because satisfaction of these rules would allow the ARA to have standing. C states the requirements of the rule.

80. Issue: Judicial Review of Administrative Agencies

The correct answer is **B.** This choice states the rule from Chevron v. NRDC (1984). A is incorrect because the Chevron rule implies deference to an agency's interpretation when the statute doesn't clearly answer the question. C is incorrect because it overstates the degree of deference owed to the agency, and ignores the rule that the court first examines whether the statute plainly answers the question. D is incorrect because the deference owed an agency's interpretation goes beyond the court determining whether the agency's construction of an ambiguous statute is the "best" one.

81. Issue: Article I Courts

The correct answer is **D.** A is incorrect because, regardless of whether the right at issue is in fact a private right, the assumption that it is a private right cuts against, not in favor of, the statute's constitutionality. B is incorrect because the "clearly erroneous" standard, the same standard used for appellate review of trial court fact-findings, is an appropriate standard for review of agency court fact-findings (see Schor v. Commodities Futures Trading Corp. (1986)). C is incorrect because there are limits on Congress' ability to place adjudication of federal claims in agency courts. D states the correct result and rationale, for the reasons explained above.

82. Issue: Standing

The correct answer is **A.** The plaintiff in B is like the plaintiffs in Lujan v. Defenders of Wildlife (1992), who argued a similar standing theory, which was rejected. The plaintiff in C is asserting a third-party standing theory of the type rejected in Warth v. Seldin (1974), on the ground that the plaintiffs' interests were only incidentally allied with those of the right-holders. The plaintiff in D is asserting a pure generalized grievance. Even though the plaintiff in A is asserting a relatively attenuated causal linkage, her claim is the strongest of these four options.

83. Issue: Dormant Commerce Clause

The correct answer is **C.** which tracks the statute struck down in West Lynn Creamery v. Healy (1994). In that case the Court found unconstitutional a statute that imposed a general tax on milk, which then funded a subsidy program for in-state milk farmers. The Court, however, found no problem with either component of this plan, finding only that their combination violated the Dormant Commerce Clause. Thus, A, B, and D are incorrect, because subsidies and neutral taxes unconnected to each other generally are constitutional.

84. Issue: Incitement and First Amendment

The correct answer is **C.** This choice correctly states the rule from Brandenburg v. Ohio (1969). A and B are incorrect, as Brandenburg requires both intent and likelihood before speech can be punished. D is incorrect because incitement speech can be punished as long as Brandenburg is satisfied.

85. Issue: Non-Delegation

The correct answer is **B.** This choice states the formula, from J.W. Hampton Co. v. United States (1927), that the Supreme Court has used ever since. A is incorrect because the rule against delegation is extremely lenient, almost to the point of non-existence. C is incorrect because Congress can give highly detailed directions to the agency if it chooses. D is incorrect because the

Supreme Court struck down two statutes on this ground in 1935 (Panama Refining v. Ryan; Schechter Poultry Corp. v. United States), and indeed has never officially overruled those cases.

86. Issue: State Sovereign Immunity

The correct answer is **C.** Because the statute includes a detailed remedial scheme, under Seminole Tribe v. Florida (1996) the Court would hold that Congress impliedly precluded Ex parte Young-type relief, such as an injunction. Thus, A is incorrect. B misstates the Young doctrine, which applies to violations of federal, not state law. D is also incorrect; the provision of the detailed remedial scheme means that Young relief is precluded, regardless of the point at which she makes the request.

87. Issue: State Sovereign Immunity

The correct answer is **D.** Of these provisions, only §5 of the Fourteenth Amendment would allow Congress to make states liable for retrospective relief. The Commerce Clause is not available (Seminole Tribe v. Florida (1996)), and the Ninth Amendment is irrelevant to this issue. Thus, the correct answer is D.

88. Issue: Congressional Power to Enforce Civil Rights

The correct answer is **A.** The basic rule from the Court's modern §5 jurisprudence is that, if the class benefiting from the legislation is a suspect class, then it is easier for Congress to make the showing necessary for it to use its §5 power (Hibbs v. Nevada Dept. of Human Resources (2003)). Sexual orientation has not been denominated a suspect class. Thus, the correct answer is A. B and C are incorrect. D is also incorrect because in §5 cases the Court engages in a more searching inquiry than that reflected by the rational basis standard.

89. Issue: Preemption

The correct answer is **D.** A is incorrect because preemption need not be based on an explicit congressional statement. B is incorrect, because it reverses the default presumption, which in fact runs against, not in favor of, a finding of preemption. C is incorrect because the fact that both statutes address the same subject matter might suggest that there may be either field or conflict preemption. For that same reason, D is correct.

90. Issue: Interstate Commerce Power

The correct answer is **B.** Employment is not necessarily itself an instrumentality of interstate commerce; rather, it is an intrastate activity that substantially affects it. Thus, A is incorrect. Because the Court applies the substantial effects test more leniently when the activity regulated is economic in nature, B is correct. C and D are incorrect because, as suggested in answer 88, it might be difficult for Congress to justify this statute as a use of its §5 power. Moreover,

Congress could not use the §5 power to regulate private parties, as the statute attempts to.

91. Issue: Anti-Commandeering

The correct answer is **B.** The statute does not commandeer state governments in the relevant sense, namely, forcing items onto the agenda of the state's decision-makers (New York v. United States (1992)). A is incorrect because commandeering has been found even when Congress regulates something that is or substantially affects interstate commerce (New York). In New York, the Court found commandeering when Congress attempted to control the activities of a state legislature; thus, C is also incorrect. D is incorrect because the Court has indicated that Congress may continue to require state courts to hear federal law causes of action (Printz v. United States (1997), explaining Testa v. Katt (1947)).

92. Issue: First Amendment Establishment Clause

The correct answer is **C.** Under Lemon v. Kurtzman (1973), a government action will violate the Establishment Clause if the statute doesn't have a secular purpose, or its principal effect is to advance or inhibit religion, or if it excessively entangles government with religion. Because any one of these criteria, if satisfied, would result in a constitutional violation, C is the correct answer. A and D are incorrect because the Court has indicated in cases such as Allegheny County v. ACLU (1989) that a combination of secular and religious displays would, if anything, make the court more, not less, likely to uphold the display. B is incorrect because intent is relevant, as noted in Lemon.

93. Issue: First Amendment Establishment Clause

The correct answer is **B.** Normally such a claim would be a generalized grievance; however, in Flast v. Cohen (1968) the Court made an exception to that standing bar for cases alleging unconstitutional government support for religion. Thus, B is the correct answer.

94. Issue: First Amendment Limits on Prior Restraints

The correct answer is **A.** Prior restraints have a heavy presumption against them, but the Court has never held that there is an absolute bar on them; thus, B and D are incorrect. C is incorrect because having a neutral decision-maker might be useful when prior government approval for speech is functionally necessary (as in the granting of a parade permit). However, it would not help in this situation, where there is no logical need for such prior approval (even if there is a compelling factual case for such prior approval).

95. Issue: Contracts Clause

The correct answer is **B.** The Contracts Clause applies only against the States, but is a part of the original Constitution, and thus wasn't incorporated through the Due Process Clause. Thus, I is part of the correct answer, but II is not.

The clause protects current contractual relationships, not prospective ones (which are protected by the Due Process Clause itself); thus, IV is part of the correct answer, but III is not. The correct combination is B.

96. Issue: Congressional Power to Enforce Civil Rights

The correct answer is **C.** Only item II is correct. The Supreme Court has held that Congress under §5 has the power to only regulate state conduct (United States v. Morrison (2000)). But it has also held that Congress' power goes farther than restating judicial rules, to prohibiting a broader swath of conduct that would effectuate enforcement of the judicial rule (Kimel v. Board of Regents (2000)). Thus, C is correct.

97. Issue: Takings

The correct answer is **B.** The public purpose requirement of the Takings Clause is quite lenient (Midkiff v. Hawaii (1984); Kelo v. City of New London (2005)), and a court will likely find that urban revitalization is a valid public purpose; thus, A is incorrect. C is incorrect because the Takings Clause does not prohibit the city from taking title; it just requires that it pay just compensation and act for a public purpose. D is incorrect, because a claim of discrimination like this would likely be weak; as long as the city had a rational basis for acting it would probably prevail. B is correct because taking title is a classic "taking" of property that would trigger the compensation requirement.

98. Issue: Political Question Doctrine

The correct answer is **C.** A is incorrect because the doctrine has nothing to do with political rights per se (Baker v. Carr (1962)). It also doesn't have anything to do with technical matters of jurisdiction; thus, B is incorrect. D is incorrect because the doctrine is concerned with clashes between branches of the federal government, not clashes between the federal government and the states (Baker). C states the correct rule from Baker.

99. Issue: Alienage Classification Under Equal Protection Clause

The correct answer is **B.** Because immigration is a federal power, Congress has more power to distinguish between aliens and citizens than the states; thus, A and C are incorrect. D is incorrect because the Supreme Court does allow the states to distinguish between aliens and citizens with regard to positions related to democratic self-government (Bernal v. Fainter (1984)). B correctly reflects these rules.

100. Issue: First Amendment Status of Libel

The correct answer is **B.** Libel itself is not protected, because by definition it is false speech. Thus, items I, III, and IV are incorrect. Only item II is correct, which makes B the correct answer. B reflects case law such as New York Times v. Sullivan (1964) that speaks to the standards of proof the First Amendment requires for libel verdicts to be consistent with the Constitution.

101. Issue: Race-Conscious Government Action Under Equal Protection Clause

The correct answer is **C**. This choice states the holding in Parents Involved v. Seattle School Dist. No. 1 (2007). A is incorrect because in Parents Involved the Court concluded that race-conscious remedial measures would normally be appropriate only when a court had adjudged the district guilty of segregation. B is incorrect because guilt would have to be formally adjudged, not unilaterally admitted years after the fact subject only to a judicial test for reasonableness. D is incorrect as the Parents Involved Court did not rely on the age of the children in reaching its holding.

102. Issue: Scope of Congressional Powers

The correct answer is **B**. I and II are both incorrect, given Seminole Tribe v. Florida (1995), which dealt with the Indian Commerce Power but which also made clear that its rule — against congressional power to make states liable for retrospective relief— applied to the Interstate Commerce Clause as well. III is part of the correct answer based on Fitzpatrick v. Bitzer (1972), which has been reaffirmed since Seminole Tribe. IV is part of the correct answer based on Central Virginia Community College v. Katz (2006), which allowed a bankruptcy trustee to recover money preferentially transferred to a state-entity creditor of the bankrupt party.

103. Issue: First Amendment Rights of Government Employees

The correct answer is **A**. This choice states the rule from Garcetti v. Ceballos (2006). In Garcetti the Court held that speech made by a government employee as part of the employee's official duties did not enjoy First Amendment protection. Thus, strict scrutiny of any government penalty for the speech is not necessary, making D incorrect. Garcetti's holding removed this speech from the normal rule applied to speech by government employees, which, as B suggests, would have required a court to inquire whether the speech was on a matter of public interest. C is incorrect because the truth or falsity of the speech was irrelevant in Garcetti's analysis.

104. Issue: Status of Second Amendment

The correct answer is **C**. This choice states the rule from District of Columbia v. Heller (2008). Heller held that the Second Amendment conferred an individual right to bear arms for self-defense, thus making A and D incorrect. B is incorrect because Heller indicated that some restrictions on gun possession, including restrictions on possession by felons and the mentally ill, would be upheld.

105. Issue: First Amendment Rights of Public School Students

The correct answer is **C**. This choice best reflects the current state of the law after Morse v. Frederick (2007). In Morse the Court upheld discipline of a student for unfurling a banner at a school event that appeared to condone drug use. The Court made clear that it was not overruling precedent recognizing that students have First Amendment rights; thus A is incorrect. However, by recognizing a school interest in suppressing student speech to combat drug use, Morse limited student speech rights; thus, B is incorrect. D is incorrect because the Court has always tied recognition of student speech rights to the special circumstances of the educational environment, and thus limited those rights as compared with the speech rights of the general public.

106. Issue: Equal Protection Challenges to Affirmative Action

The correct answer is **A.** This choice restates the approach the Court took in Grutter v. Bollinger (2003), in which the Court deferred to the Law School's argument that racial diversity improved the educational experience. B is incorrect because even though the Court said it was performing strict scrutiny, its deference to the school amounted to less than a searching inquiry. C and D are both incorrect because the Court has rejected claims that educational affirmative action is justified by a desire to remedy general societal discrimination.

107. Issue: Congressional Power Under the Interstate Commerce Power

The correct answer is **C.** This choice restates the reasoning in Gonzalez v. Raich (2005). A is incorrect, given the "leakage" argument the Court accepted in Raich. B is incorrect because Congress does not have the power to legislate for the general welfare, although it does have power to tax and spend for the general welfare. D is incorrect; given congressional power as construed in Raich, this would not be one of those few regulatory areas completely reserved to the states.

108. Issue: Congressional Power Under the Interstate Commerce Power

The correct answer is **C.** This choice reflects how the Court approached the effect of the analogous California medical marijuana law in Raich. The Court held that Congress could rationally conclude that the state law would not fully prevent medically prescribed marijuana from leaking into the interstate market, thus making A incorrect. The fact that Congress only had to have a rational basis for believing in the possibility of leakage makes D incorrect. This also makes B incorrect; all Congress needed was a rational basis for believing in the possibility of leakage in order for the Court to uphold federal power, regardless of how attenuated the effects of Tom's conduct interstate commerce were.

109. Issue: Establishment Clause Limits on Government Display of Religious Texts and Monuments

The correct answer is **C.** This choice best conveys the state of the law after Van Orden v. Perry (2005), on which this question is based. A is incorrect because it is far too strict a test; many government displays convey a religious message without thereby running afoul of the Establishment Clause. B is incorrect because it is also too broad: a religious paining hung in a government-owned museum is owned by the government but the government's display of the painting does not violate the Establishment Clause. D is incorrect because it is essentially the mirror image of A. C best states the analysis in Van Orden, in which a plurality noted the dual religious and secular meaning of the monument and on that basis upheld its placement against an Establishment Clause challenge.

110. Issue: The Equal Protection "Class of One" Theory

The correct answer is **C.** This choice restates the rule from the 2000 case of Village of Willowbrook v. Olech. In Olech the Court allowed the plaintiffs to go forward with a lawsuit charging a town with violating their equal protection rights based on facts similar to those in this question. In Olech the plaintiffs had a spat with the town they lived in, after which the town demanded a larger-than-usual easement over the plaintiffs' property to hook them up to the town's utility system. The plaintiffs sued alleging that the town had singled them out for bad treatment and thereby violated their equal protection rights. In allowing the suit to go forward, the Court concluded that equal protection plaintiffs did not need to allege that they were the victim of discrimination based on membership in a particular class, say, as Asians or women. Thus, answer A is incorrect. Moreover, the Court concluded that the plaintiffs did not need to show any subjective ill intent on the part of the defendants; only that the defendants acted without a rational basis. Thus, answer B is incorrect and answer C is correct. Finally, Olech dealt with the same sort of petty land-use dispute as the sort at issue in this question; the fact that the Court allowed the suit to go forward means that answer D is also incorrect.

111. Issue: The Equal Protection "Class of One" Theory

The correct answer is **D.** This choice restates the result in a follow-up to the Olech case discussed above, the 2008 case of Engquist v. Oregon Dept of Agriculture. In that case the plaintiff was a government employee who alleged she was fired based on her employer's dislike of her, thus violating her equal protection rights. The Court dismissed the claim on the theory that the class-of-one theory did not apply in the workplace. Thus, answers A and B are incorrect. Answer C is incorrect because Village of Willowbrook v. Olech (2000) allows claims based on membership in a "class of one" — i.e., claims that don't require that the discrimination was based on membership in a larger class such as the disabled or Latinos. However, the Court refused to extend that theory into claims by government employees, therefore making D the correct answer.

112. Issue: The First Amendment and Compelled Speech and Association

The correct answer is **B.** These specialized taxes for marketing programs raise First Amendment concerns because they may amount to government coercing the taxpayer to fund and thus associate with speech with which he disagrees. Thus, A understates the taxpayer's First Amendment interest and is incorrect. At the other extreme, however, the only way government can pay for speech is with tax revenues; thus, D overstates the taxpayer's First Amendment interest and is also incorrect. C is incorrect because if the court concludes that the speech is the government's own then any forced association with the speech is mitigated and the First Amendment injury disappears. B is the correct answer. The Court has held that, despite the First Amendment concerns in these types of programs, if the speech is merely part of a general marketing or production scheme then the First Amendment concern is mitigated, and the government's interest in having an effective program via encouraging consumption of the product justifies the intrusion on the taxpayer's speech and association concerns. Conversely, if marketing and production facets of the program are absent then the taxpayer's First Amendment interests carry more weight.

113. Issue: First Amendment Limits on Campaign Finance Regulation

The correct answer is **B.** The same First Amendment rules apply to states and the federal government; thus, D is incorrect. A is incorrect because the Court has always recognized that campaign expenditures and contributions include at least some element of expression. Even contributions signal one's support for a candidate and thus count as speech. C is incorrect because the Court has concluded that the most expressive part of a campaign contribution is the simple fact of making a contribution. A larger contribution may signal more intense support but ultimately restrictions on the size of contributions burden relatively little speech, thus allowing some campaign contribution restrictions. B is correct because it states this rule.

114. Issue: The Fourteenth Amendment Privileges and Immunities Clause

The correct answer is **B.** This choice states the rule from the Slaughter-House Cases (1873). In those cases the Court gave a very narrow reading to this clause, to protect only the privileges and immunities of "national citizenship." The Court rejected the argument that it protects a broad array of liberty interests; thus A is incorrect. D is incorrect because the strict scrutiny rule for racial classifications ultimately became grounded in the Equal Protection Clause. C is incorrect because the rule against discriminating against out-of-staters is found in the Privileges and Immunities Clause of Article IV, not the similarly worded clause in the Fourteenth Amendment.

115. Issue: The Fourteenth Amendment Right to Vote

The correct answer is **C.** D is incorrect because Baker v. Carr (1962) held this issue to not constitute a political question. In Reynolds v. Sims the Court required something close to equality in the population size represented by each state district in a given legislative chamber; thus, A is incorrect. B is incorrect because in Reynolds the Court explicitly rejected analogizing upper houses of state legislatures to the United States Senate, where the equal representation of states means that both populous states are effectively underrepresented. Reynolds' requirement of nearly equally sized legislative districts is reflected in answer C.